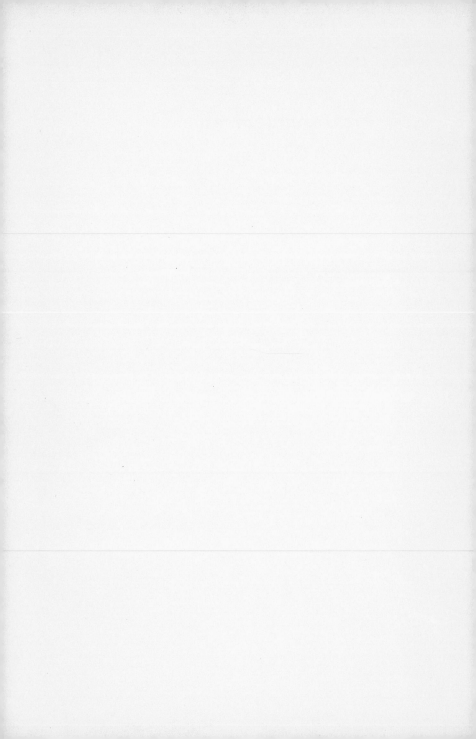

Explication as
Criticism

Explication as Criticism

✻

Selected Papers from the
English Institute
1941 - 1952

EDITED WITH A FOREWORD BY

W. K. Wimsatt, Jr.

✻

COLUMBIA UNIVERSITY PRESS
NEW YORK AND LONDON 1963

Foreword

NEARLY all of the sixty-four "eager scholars" who registered for the inaugural English Institute in 1939 are still alive. Yet the origins and initial aims of the Institute, somewhat sketchily committed to print in the first few *Annuals,* may already begin to seem obscure. Professor Rudolf Kirk, who, in virtue of his having edited the first four volumes of the *Institute Annual* and having written the prefaces of the second, third, and fourth volumes, may be looked on as the earliest historian of the Institute, tells us that it was "first conceived and outlined" by "two plotters" in a "Greenwich Village restaurant, January 27, 1938" (1942 Preface). And he pays a warm testimony to the "leadership" of Professor Carleton Brown, Chairman of the Supervising Committee for the first two years— the eminent medievalist who in 1934 had retired after fifteen years as Secretary of the Modern Language Association of America and who had been President of the Association in 1936. "Without Carleton Brown, the English Institute would not exist" (1940 Preface). Carleton Brown died in June, 1941. The aim of the English Institute, according to its first program, was to discuss "basic problems in the philosophy and technique of research, as distinct from discussion of specified subject matter" (1941 Preface). In an introduction written specially for the *English Institute Annual, 1939,* Professor Robert E. Spiller spoke at length of a kind of "restlessness" which seemed to pervade the profession of English scholarship in that era— "a stirring in our profession toward new outlets of thought and work." And he viewed this stirring as "in a sense, the sequel of the semi-centennial meeting of the Modern Language Association of 1933." Both Carleton Brown, on the "eve of his retirement" as Secretary of the Association, and Professor John Livingston Lowes, the President of that year 1933, had delivered addresses which in 1939 were still vividly remembered. "If we can infuse the gains of our mastered technique with some measure of the ampler spirit of our earlier days," Professor Lowes had concluded, "our scholarship will be not one whit less scientific, but both in itself and in its influence, more humane." "The hiatus between our reported facts and our creative criticism," said Professor Spiller in one of his own variations on the theme, "has been too great." He alluded to a kind of "bondage" to philological specialization which had made "much of our work impeccably accurate and completely inconsequential."

The war had something to do with the founding of the Institute. It was "projected," said Professor Kirk, "amid rumours of war" (1941 Preface). And in that summer of 1939, as Professor Brown in his foreword to the first *Annual* observes, the outbreak of war had imposed an "embargo" on the annual exodus of American scholars to the European libraries. It seems extravagant in retrospect, but that first gathering of the Institute, in South Hall, the new library building, at Columbia University, continued for nearly two full weeks, August 28 to September 9, 1939. The sixty-four eager registrants had an opportunity of hearing and discussing twenty-four morning papers (in four series—I. English and American Dialects; II. Editing Middle English Texts; III. Editing Correspondences; IV. The Social Backgrounds of Drama). They could hear no fewer than nine evening lectures, by as many learned speakers, on such business-like topics as "Finding Literary Documents" (J. M. Osborn), "The Selection of Graduate Students" (Howard Mumford Jones), "The Historical Records Survey and Literary Scholarship" (Luther H. Evans), "The Publishing of Research" (F. W. Bateson), "Choosing a Topic for Research" (Carl Van Doren).

The gathering of the second year, reduced to the more plausible duration of a week, was once more devoted mainly to a hard-core program (Folk Speech and Culture, Dating of Books by Bibliographical Evidence, The Rare Book Library, Dealer and Collector, Copyright Laws, Type Design for the Scholarly Book), but at the same time appeared the first outright concession to "Literary Criticism," a program of speculative papers by William Y. Tindall, David Daiches, Cleanth Brooks, Allen Tate, and W. H. Auden. The conferences of this year are said to have produced "heated discussion" (1940 Preface). In the third year a program entitled "Literary Criticism: The Interpretation of Poetry" inaugurated for the Institute the novel theme of "explication." Norman Holmes Pearson was the Chairman. Papers by Horace Gregory, Lionel Trilling, Cleanth Brooks, and Frederick A. Pottle showed four ways of thinking about Wordsworth's "Ode: Intimations of Immortality from Recollections of Early Childhood."

Pearl Harbor came soon after. A fourth meeting of the Institute was contracted to the three days of the Labor Day weekend of 1942 and was in the event partly makeshift. The Institute then disappeared for the space of three years.

On the resumption of the meetings at Columbia in September, 1946 (the number of registrants swelling to 169), the program embraced two series of papers which for the first time in the history of the Institute so closely complemented each other that the editors for the year could put together a volume that centered upon a critical idea. "With interrelated themes," ventured the editors modestly, "these essays should prove valuable to all who are interested in modern literary criticism." The two series were Professor Gerald E. Bentley's on "The Critical Significance of Biographical Evidence" and Professor Arthur Mizener's on "The Methods of Literary Studies." Some of the papers in the second series, as it happened, illustrated the theme of the first with surprising cogency. The concept of biography in relation to literary criticism

is one which readily expands into the more general
concept of historical information in relation to criticism. With its first postwar program, of 1946, the Institute for the first time in earnest and with a great
measure of accuracy addressed itself to discussing that
hiatus between "our reported facts and our creative
criticism" which Professor Spiller had regretted in
1939, that humanizing of the scholar's "mastered technique" which Professor Lowes had even earlier desired.

Annual volumes of essays selected from those read
at the Institute had from the start reflected the har-
moniously bipartisan makeup of the Institute and its
programs, dividing their tables of contents as fairly
as possible between the more humane and the more
technical papers. After the relative anomaly of the
thematic volume of 1946, the earlier trend reestab-
lished itself. The annual English Institute volume of
essays was in short a miscellany. In 1953 the Institute
Supervising Committee and the editors of the Columbia University Press joined in the view that a
more coherent annual volume was desirable. A small
volume of partly borrowed essays on Ezra Pound was
the result in the same year. The present editor had
the pleasure of presenting in the next year the first
thematically unified volume composed entirely of
English Institute essays, under the title of *English
Stage Comedy*.

The volume which I now present is an attempt to
return to the earlier period of Institute essays, 1939–

43, 1946–52, and to bring together from them a collection of related papers. Certainly it is not my opinion that the only good essays during the first eleven years of the Institute are the explicatory. Brilliant essays of diverse sorts beckon from every volume—to mention but a few for which I have a special fondness: Osborn's on "The Search for Literary Documents," 1939; Wellek's on "Literary Movements and Periods," 1940, and on "The Parallelism between Literature and the Arts," 1941; Stevens's "Imagination as Value," 1948; Frye's "Argument of Comedy," 1948; Abrams's "Wordsworth and Coleridge on Diction and Figures," 1952. The essays in explication reprinted in the present volume have been selected because in themselves each is distinguished and each is representative of important aims of the Institute, and because taken together they constitute a coherent image of the Institute's effort for the integration of historical knowledge and critical thinking. They make, I believe, the most coherent single volume which could have been devised from the varied wealth of materials available. I have ventured to put a theoretical effort of my own, 1951, in an introductory position.

Historical knowledge and critical thinking. The essays brought together in this volume form a remarkable collection if only in their repeated and varied illustration of that union. Next to the high standard of their critical expertise, the most striking character of these essays is the variety and thoroughness of the several kinds of knowledge brought to play in the explicative purpose—the philology of the old, tough kind (our "mastered technique") needed to understand the "popular idiom" of the *Miller's Tale,* the Elizabethan music (broken consort, alarum, tucket, and air) discovered as an accent of Shakespeare's Trojan satirical tragedy, the Aristotelian philosophy of imitated "action" invoked for a perspective upon *Macbeth,* the political and military history of the Commonwealth enlisted to show how Marvell's Ode to Cromwell transcends such history, the realities of English foreign policy and of engravers' techniques expounded in support of the "visions" of Blake, the psychological finesse exercised in a definition of Wordsworth's "visionary gleam." Professor Douglas Bush's essay on Milton is an exception to the prevailing pattern, yet a relevant one: it is not an explication but a statement about certain ways in which historical (biographical) knowledge need not enter the explication of the poet's poems.

The title of this volume, taken from my introductory essay, asserts that explication *is* criticism; it *is* the evaluative account of the poem. Even those philosophies of criticism which profess least concern for explication are likely to find themselves at moments betrayed into recognizing that explication is inescapable. Yet in a more special sense the school of "explication" which arose in America during the 1940s and which continues so energetically today can lay claim to a superior understanding and employ-

ment of the explicative faculty. One reason for this,
a master reason, lies in the kind of perspective implied in the liberal explicative approach to poetry.
This may be indicated succinctly in a formulation
made by one of the fathers of modern explication,
Professor I. A. Richards, in his *Practical Criticism* of
1929. Richards wanted to test poems by considering
them ("passing them through the mind") within a
certain "frame of feelings"—feelings "whose sincerity
is beyond our questioning." The feelings, nevertheless,
had to be defined in terms of the objects of contemplation which aroused them. To these relics of the middle years of the generation which founded the English
Institute I would now for a moment return. They
are, said Richards, "i. Man's loneliness (the isolation
of the human situation). ii. The facts of birth, and of
death, in their inexplicable oddity. iii. The incon-
ceivable immensity of the Universe. iv. Man's place
in the perspective of time. v. The enormity of his
ignorance" (1935, p. 290). The significance of this
frame of reference for Richards was that it was a key
to "sincerity" of feeling. Let me venture, in a more
cognitive idiom, that the importance of the statement
is that it describes a frame of reference which is both
objective (a reality beyond and greater than the
visionary poet himself and his critic) and at the same
time sufficiently abstract—that is, ultimate and hu-
manly irreducible, transcending the mythopoeic formulations. Thus, although it *is* a highly abstract
frame of reference, it permits or promotes a maxi-

mum concreteness, finesse, and flexibility in the
critic's coming in from the circumference to the actuality of poems themselves. It permits and promotes an
activity of literary criticism both variously specific and
coherently ordered, both free and disciplined—aimed
but not arbitrary.

The eight essays which compose this volume were
published originally by the Columbia University
Press in the *English Institute Annual, 1941,* and *English Institute Essays, 1946, 1950, 1951, 1952.* Several
of the essays have been reprinted in other places. The
present volume uses the English Institute texts, with
only a few small corrections, a few added notes
(dated), and a few silent omissions of details relevant
only to the original contexts. It is a pleasure to express my thanks to the authors for their permission to
reprint the essays and for their help with the texts.

W. K. W., Jr.

Silliman College, Yale University
January 24, 1963

Contents

Foreword, BY W. K. WIMSATT, JR.   vii

Explication as Criticism, 1951,
   BY W. K. WIMSATT, JR.   1

Idiom of Popular Poetry in the *Miller's Tale,*
   1950, BY E. T. DONALDSON   27

Troilus and Cressida: Music for the Play, 1952,
   BY FREDERICK W. STERNFELD   53

Macbeth as the Imitation of an Action, 1951,
   BY FRANCIS FERGUSSON   85

Literary Criticism: Marvell's "Horatian Ode,"
   1946, BY CLEANTH BROOKS   99

John Milton, 1946, BY DOUGLAS BUSH   131

Blake; the Historical Approach, 1950,
   BY DAVID V. ERDMAN   147

Worthsworth's "Ode: Intimations of
   Immortality," 1941, BY LIONEL TRILLING   175

Explication as Criticism

Explication as Criticism

✳

By W. K. WIMSATT, Jr.

MY AIM in this paper is to talk about the question whether explication of a poem is itself an act of criticism and hence of evaluation. Not whether it is necessary to understand a poem in order to criticize it (the question in that form is little better than rhetorical), but whether to understand a poem is the same as to criticize it. This, indeed, I conceive to be the only critical question that can be asked about explication. And this is far from a rhetorical question. The correct answer to it lies, I believe, not in a simple affirmation or denial, but in an adjustment. My effort to give an answer will move toward a "monism" of criticism or evaluation through explication, but it will insist at the same time on certain other principles.

As both the method and the philosophy of explicative criticism are very strongly established in our day, it has seemed to me easiest to make my own approach to the philosophy in the direction of its difficulties. I find my own account of explication caught constantly between certain opposed pairs of ideas, and these will be my main topics of discussion—namely, (1) part and whole, or the rival claims of these entities to critical consideration; (2) value and disvalue, or the difficulty of describing disvalue in a philosophy of value which rises above the pleasure principle; (3) value and neutrality, or the difficulty of uniting evaluation with what we commonly think of as the neutral facts. Accompanying these pairs and tending to involve and unite them and hence to appear in one way or another at all points of the discussion is a fourth pair, the explicit and the implicit—or the difference between them, yet their interdependence in the meaning of the poem. In the course of an attempt to show that these four pairs of ideas are to be considered as coming inside the theory of explication, I shall have occasion to inquire if another pair, the affective and the cognitive, are to be considered in the same way.

The thesis that explication is criticism, or is at least immediately and intimately related to criticism, proceeds quite reasonably from any theory of poetry which sees the poem as an organized whole—a wholeness of vision, that is, established through wholeness of diverse, but reconciled, parts. And this is more or less true no matter whether the kind of "holism" invoked be the realistic and Aristotelian, the idealistic (either neo-Platonic or romantic subjective), or the affective, the synesthesis of Richards—although, as I hinted a moment ago, the course of our argument may develop certain relevant differences among these theories. The success of explication in persuading us of literary value is a kind of practical test of how well aesthetic theories of order and wholeness do apply to literary works. More specifically, a practical affinity between holism and explication arises because organization and wholeness are matters of structure and hence also of implication. Organization and wholeness are at stake, for instance, when we ask what kind of coherence actually obtains between two parts of an *Extasie,* one part mystical, the other apparently seductive. It is not clear to me, indeed, that Dryden, in providing a motto for the organ of our guild—"The last verse is not yet sufficiently explicated"—had in mind more than the explication of the explicit. But the explicator will surely not conceive that he has employed his talent to the full unless he performs not only that service (as in glosses and other linguistic and historical observations) but also the explicitation of the implicit. For poetry is never altogether, or even mainly, "poetry of statement." The very difference between those two sides of the explicable, the explicit and the implicit, and the ways in which one may relate to the other are matters with which the explicator will be deeply engaged.

One of the difficulties of explicative holism arises in one form or another from what we may roughly describe as the competition of parts with whole. Holistic theories of beauty have always had difficulty in coping with the fact that such simple things as bright colors and sweet sounds are usually called beautiful, the fact that our idea of beauty usually does begin with such experiences and persists naïvely in including them, except in the face of the most studious self-denial. As the sophist Hippias was made to remark, "Gold is a beautiful thing." One escape from the equivocation thus apparently arising for the term "beauty" is the assignment of the name "pleasant" or "agreeable" (the Kantian *Angenehm*) to such simpler experiences, the name "beauty" being reserved for the higher and more complex. A bright color or a note on a French horn will be pleasant; painting or music, beautiful. Another kind of escape, however, and one I believe to be of more interest to us as literary theorists, was that provided by the neo-Platonic and medieval aesthetic of the luminous, and to some extent by its parallel the aesthetic of numerical harmony.[1] The latter of these, proceeding on Pythagorean and Platonic conceptions concerning relations between mathematics, music, and astronomy (the affinities of the *Quadrivium*), arrived at a synthesis of beauty in order and unity with far less of an analogical leap. The aesthetic of the luminous was more daring and solved a bigger difficulty, saying in effect that the reason we apply the term "beautiful" to simple bright things and to complex harmonies alike is the Platonic reason that light is an analogue of intelligible reality —light is to the eye as truth is to the mind. The radiant color of a Byzantine mosaic or of a painting of saints by Fra Angelico is an analogue of the ordered brilliance of the whole composition. The doctrine has a close relation to the equally ancient doctrine that sight, along with hearing, is a chief aesthetic sense— a sense that can understand things—not just be stimulated by them or amorphously rubbed against them.

[1] See Edgar de Bruyne, *Études d'esthétique médiévale,* Bruges, 1946, Tome III, Livre IV, ch. 1, "L'Esthétique de la lumière."

It is a doctrine which is echoed in our own inevitable habits of aesthetic praise, our metaphoric vocabulary of positive evaluation—not "dirty," "drab," "muddy," or "dark," but "clean," "bright," "radiant," "fiery," "brilliant," "gorgeous," "orchidaceous." And we are likely to feel that with these terms of approval we are doing more justice to the worth of the poem than if we were to say it is smooth or sweet.

When Plotinus devised his own expression of the theory which I have just sketched, in the sixth essay of his first *Ennead,* he did so in order to refute a notion which seemed to him implied in the Stoic theory of symmetry, that the parts of a pattern can have beauty only in virtue of their relation to the whole. And in this, perhaps, the relevance of the ancient problem to our own thinking can be most readily seen. For one of the most persistent implications of holism and ex-plicationism is that the parts do have value only as interacting and making the whole. And this is an article of the philosophy which is bound to impose some hard work here and there on the explicator— even when he is working on very exquisitely finished poems. Perhaps the difficulty of eliciting the signif-icance of every detail will be the greater in proportion to the largeness and greatness of the poem. Extreme holism is obviously contrary to our experience of literature. We do not wait until the end of the play or novel to know whether the first scene or chapter is brilliant or dull—no long work, in fact, would ever be witnessed or read if this were so. A poem, said Coleridge, the father of holism in English criticism, is a composition which proposes "to itself such delight from the whole, as is compatible with a distinct gratification from each component part." [2] The value of a whole poem, while undoubtedly reflecting something back to the parts, has to grow out of parts which are themselves valuable. *The Rape of the Lock* would not come off were not the couplets witty. We may add that good poems may have dull parts; bad poems, bright parts. How minutely this principle could be applied without arriving at a theory of Longinian "sudden flashes," of "cathartically charged images," of Arnoldian touchstones, of poetic diction, or of irrelevant local texture I do not know; nor what the minimal dimension of wit or local brilliance of structure may be; nor to what extent a loosely constructed whole may be redeemed by the energy of individual chapters or scenes. Yet the validity of partial value as a general principle in tension with holism seems obvious. The whole with which explication is concerned is something elastic and approximate.

And yet what I have just been saying is not true in the sense that the poetic part could ever be literally like the bright color or the sweet sound of our direct experience. Of all the branches of aesthetics, poetic theory most easily disposes of the competition between part and whole which we have been describing. For poetry entertains no beautiful ideas or words as such. Its materials, unlike those of sculpture, do not have to be high-class—marble or diorite. They include

2 *Biographia literaria,* ed. by Shawcross, II, 10.

everything, "the weariness, the fever, and the fret," dung, poison, pain, deformity, and death. All, we are convinced, may be assimilated by the peculiar process of the given poem. Poetry is the art which most readily transcends the simple pleasure principle and illustrates the principle of structure and harmonious tension.

For somewhat the same reason, however, poetic theory appears to me to be that branch of aesthetic theory which has the greatest difficulty with a certain other obstacle to synthesis—"disvalue." [3] I mean, not the absence only of value, a vacuum, and not merely an inferior value, a minor pattern of order, but actual disvalue—sources of displeasure in our reading of bad poetry or pseudo-poetry; and not only in local blemishes or partial defects but also in total structures, poems which are wholly bad. The aesthetic of harmonious order is closely related to an ontology which sees evil in general, and hence ugliness, as a special kind of negative, an absence or privation where something is needed to fill out a harmony. The meaning of this doctrine is most easily realized in such examples as a man without an eye or a leg or a kidney. But even here our realization of disvalue comes about most readily through our very positive sense of the inconvenient and the painful. Sheer disvalue in an onto-

[3] A recent note on this topic, Lucius Garvin's "The Problem of Ugliness in Art," *The Philosophical Review*, LVII (July, 1948), 404–409, testifies once more to its capacity to introduce confusion. The term "disvalue" is not, so far as I know, in current use. I choose it in preference to "ugliness" or "badness" as being more generic and less familiar—hence less concretely committed in certain awkward directions.

logical sense, complete substantive chaos or disorder, is not conceivable. Anything that is anything at all has a minimal kind of order and being. Our experience of the painful, the evil, and the ugly is not actually negative—the knife in the dark, the cunning plot, the riotous passion, the distorted countenance. If their evil lies in a deviation from a fullness and rightness of human nature, it is none the less powered by a violent positive activity of the human substance. Yet poetry, as we have noted, transcends and subsumes all this evil and by perspective makes it part of aesthetic value. So we might think of poetry, the reflection of the universe and its intensification through our spirit's activity, as the art in which the ontological principle would be most easily realized—where indeed, as Keats yearned to experience, the ideal would be the real and there would be no disvalue—only greater and lesser values; only expression and lack of expression. A good poem, we have often heard, is simply a real poem, a genuine poem. And on this theory of value, how could we ever explicate disvalue? Would not a very bad poem, on this theory, be simply one about which we can say very little or nothing at all?

Perhaps we ought to begin by confessing that many poems which we are accustomed to call bad, or at least about which we are accustomed to profess discomfort, are not actually bad, but only less good. The element of discomfort attached to them may be a part of our snobbery—or it may come through a reflexive light cast upon the author's vanity or obtuseness. If he had not professed to write a poem, if he had not called it a poem and printed it on fine paper, the offense might be far less.

Our escape, however, will hardly be complete that way. It will remain to advert to a fact of more critical importance: that is, the peculiar way in which two kinds of truth, that of assertion or correspondence (the accent of explicitness) and that of structure or coherence (the accent of implication) are united in verbal discourse and depend on each other. The simplest kind of verbal assertion (let us say "hawthorn is white") if it is true has a truth both of correspondence and of coherence. The whole expression corresponds to reality; but looked at internally and verbally, this correspondence consists of a coherence between subject and predicate. They go together. Poetry is a complex kind of verbal construction in which the dimension of coherence is by various techniques of implication greatly enhanced and thus generates an extra dimension of correspondence to reality, the symbolic or analogical. But all this structure of meaning rises upon a certain element of unavoidably direct reference to outside reality and upon at least a minimal truth of such reference.

If it were otherwise, then indeed would poetry achieve the status of a pure idealism. Elements of falsity could scarcely creep into the poet's discourse. Poetry could not go wrong. Everything the poet said would simply have more or less being or character and be more or less valuable. Some such idealistic assumption or desire surely prompted Leibnitz to the remark

quoted with approval by Herder: "I like almost everything I read." [4] A kind of inversion of that assumption,
but equally simplistic, could produce in Tolstoy the
view that clarity of meaning is so much a characteristic
of sincerity and of moral value that the unintelligibil-
ity of Baudelaire was almost the same thing as his im-
morality.[5] A more cautious neo-Platonic statement was
that of Joubert, that clarity "is so eminently one of the
characteristics of truth, that often it even passes for
truth itself." [6]

The response of reality to verbal expression, while
to some extent elastic and plastic (we can in some sense
see best what we can best express) is at the same time
in very important ways obdurate and recalcitrant. The
elasticity comes in the nexus which obtains between
words and things, one by which words can be twisted
and stretched a long way and yet maintain a coherence
and validity of their own—as long as the referential
relation to reality is not entirely broken. A theory of
poetic wholeness and coherence need not proceed to
the extreme—either idealistic or positivistic—of mak-

[4] "Niemand hat weniger Censorgeist als ich habe. Sonderbar ists;
aber mir gefällt das Meiste was ich lese . . . ich bin einmal so ge-
bauet, dass ich allenthalben am liebsten aufsuche und bemerke, was
Lobenswerth ist, nicht was Tadel verdienet."—Herder, "Briefe zu
Beförderung der Humanität," 1795, in his *Werke,* ed. by B. Suphan,
XVII, 338. I am indebted for this quotation to my colleague Professor René Wellek.
[5] Chapter X of Tolstoy's *What Is Art?* never actually makes that
equation, but drives very hard toward it. In another essay, his Introduction to the works of Maupassant, Tolstoy faces the facts
better when he finds Maupassant highly intelligible, but is willing
to call him at the same time immoral.
[6] Matthew Arnold, "Joubert," *Essays in Criticism, First Series,* London, 1902, p. 282.

ing the only kind of untruth the unmeaningful. The kind of truth found in poetry (if either our poetry or our criticism is to survive) will have to be more than the satisfaction aroused by the contemplation of a system of symbols. Most of us are in fact very practically equipped to resist this kind of total submersion of knowledge into the dimension of coherence. The routine technique of our historical studies may often induce us into writing a defense of some mean work of literature just because we have come to understand the conventions according to which it was written. But we do not really think that way. We know all along that some historically understandable things are wicked or silly.

Active or positive disvalue in poetry arises when some abstractly true assertion or correct attitude is blurred or garbled in symbolic or stylistic incoherencies or (more flagrantly) when some false assertion or attitude is inflated into a specious form of coherence. A sentimental, that is, an excessive or oversimplified, feeling about an object can be endowed, for instance, with such a pattern of coherence and suggestion of deep resonance as the metrical and rhyming scheme of a sonnet. The very fact that a poem is a sonnet may create a greater opportunity for badness than if it were a free-verse ramble. Or again, a poem can be given an illusion of depth by the introduction of apparently real, but actually phantasmal or irrelevant, symbols. In such cases explication reveals disvalue by explicating the absence of the truly explicable. In such cases there is more (and less) than mere lack or meagerness of meaning. There is the positive and active carelessness and self-deception of the human will and imagination. This is disvalue, and from it comes our experience of displeasure.[7]

It is a curious testimony to the inseparability of the topics which I have proposed to discuss in this paper that the difficulty concerning disvalue which we have just seen, along with such solution as I may have provided, greatly facilitates the illustration of what I conceive to be the chief validity and advantage of a fully explicative criticism—though I must ask your patience in waiting a short time before I can bring these ideas together. The greatest advantage in keeping our explicative activity as close as possible to our evaluative is that we thereby escape the sundering of minds and hence in the end the destruction of critical discourse, which come about through affective ways of talking about poems—ways which emphasize our minds exactly so far as they are individual agents reacting to impulses and moving in separation. The issue is not always clearly recognized; it is often disguised by a terminology of ends and means. Thus Professor David Daiches, in his *Study of Literature for Readers and Critics:*

[7] If we care to strengthen our feeling of distaste for a bad poem by invoking the guilty personality of the poet himself, we may do so in the words of Yvor Winters: "One feels, whether rightly or wrongly, a correlation between the control evinced within a poem and the control within the poet behind it." *Primitivism and Decadence,* New York, 1937, p. 7.

Pattern by itself does not make literature; it must be the kind of pattern which communicates insight. A mistake made by many contemporary critics, particularly in the discussion of poetry, is to regard subtlety or complexity of arrangement as itself a criterion of literary·worth. But pattern in literature is a means to an end, not an end in itself.[8]

But in literature a part is never a means to another part which is the end or to a whole which is the end— unless in the organistic sense that all parts and the whole are reciprocally ends and means, the heart, the head, and the hand. The end-means relation in literature (so far as the end is outside the means) is a relation between us the readers and the poem by means of which the poet, indeed, may be aiming at us. Inside the poem there are no ends and means, only whole and parts.

The affective theory of I. A. Richards, or the affective side of his theory, was implicitly an end-means theory about poetry as a means of working on us— except that here and there this theory got mixed up with a cognitive part-whole terminology, as in the following single sentence of his chapter "The Language of Criticism." "This trick of judging the whole by the detail . . . of mistaking the means for the end, the technique for the value, is in fact much the most successful of the snares which waylay the critic." [9] I suggest that the separation of technique from value which results from confusing means and end with part and whole was in the case of Mr. Richards a far more suc-

[8] Page 80.
[9] *Principles of Literary Criticism,* New York, 1934, p. 24.

cessful snare. It was the resolute unification of technique and value, of knowledge and value, in the system of Croce which provoked the sneering remarks about him in the early books of Richards. And Croce's idealism is, indeed, one plausible, though extreme, terminus of the cognitive tendency in criticism—a unification of reality and mind so thorough that all is united in one, the absolute reality of spirit. Yet Croce's system, so far as it is not explicitly anti-analytic—and in his later amendments and in his practical demonstrations it is not—actually promotes explication,[10] simply because it does insist on the poem as an act of knowledge.

But the rift between technique and value accomplished by Richards's *Principles of Literary Criticism* appeared most clearly and curiously in the chapter on "Badness in Poetry." And it is here that we may see disvalue (with its inherently divisive tendency) as a severe test of just how coherently cognitive a theory of poems may be. There were in Mr. Richards's system two kinds of bad poems: one, illustrated by a tiny scrap of H. D.'s imagism (*The Pool*), in which the "original experience" was somehow recognized to have "had some value," although there was a serious failure to communicate the value; and the other, illustrated by a heavy-footed sonnet of Ella Wheeler Wilcox's on love and friendship, in which the re-

[10] See for instance his analytic description of a passage in Virgil's *Aeneid* in the *Britannica* article "Aesthetics." I am told that such explications abound in several of his latest and untranslated volumes—for instance, in *Poesia antica e moderna, interpretazioni,* Bari, 1940, and *Letture di poeti,* Bari, 1950.

production of "the state of mind of the writer" was thought to be very exact, although the values thus reproduced or communicated were sadly inferior. It is to be noted in passing that this kind of division in badness produced an especially mysterious instance of what I call "intentionalism." How could he tell that H. D.'s poem proceeded from a valuable experience? [11] But the more important thing to note is that once the merit of perfect communication (that is, expression and hence structure and meaning) was conceded to the sonnet by Ella Wheeler Wilcox, there was no way left of explaining how it was bad. Mr. Richards spoke of the "pleasure and admiration" which ensue for many readers from "the soothing effect of aligning the very active Love-Friendship groups of impulses with so settled yet rich a group as the Summer-Autumn simile brings in." "The value of the reconciliation," he said, "depends upon the level of organization at which it takes place, upon whether the reconciled impulses are adequate or inadequate. In this case those who have adequate impulses . . . are not appeased. Only for those who make certain conventional, stereotyped maladjustments instead, does the magic work." [12] My objection to this as a critique of the poem is that instead of talking about the poem to you or to me, Mr. Richards backed off and started talking equally about the poem and about you and me—what it was going to do to our impulses if they were set

[11] Unless by something like "stock responses" to a vocabulary of vitality, sensation, and outdoor nature.
[12] Page 202.

in a certain way; what if not. Those remarks about our adequate or inadequate impulses were an opaque substitute for a discourse that could easily have focussed an embarrassing light on the poem itself. What kind of love was it (not Cupid, one assumed; not Venus) who had managed to "lead" us by an action composed entirely of "his own throes and torments, and desires"? Did this allegorical figure, appearing so strangely in a landscape of midsummer burned to ashes, stand for something inside us or for something outside? What kind of love had we experienced anyway? Why, indeed, were we haunted with a sense of loss? Not only the "triteness" of the close, as Mr. Richards put it, but its fatuity was to be noted. In short, what was wrong with the poem was that neither in its main explicit statement nor in the implications of its imagistic parts (and of its overemphatic metrical pattern) did it make sense.[13] In some such manner, the criticism of this poem might have been much more closely unified with a criticism of the first, even though one might wish to insist that while neither poem actually conveyed anything very coherent, the second was more offensive because it made an elaborate pretense of doing so.

We have now arrived at a point in our argument where it is convenient to introduce a final and, as it

[13] A single sentence of Mr. Richards's critique was technical and cognitive. "The heavy regular rhythm, the dead stamp of the rimes, the obviousness of the descriptions ("mellow, mild, St. Martin"; "cool, verdant vales"), their alliteration, the triteness of the close, all these accentuate the impression of conclusiveness" (p. 201).

appears to me, the most troublesome difficulty that confronts a philosophy of explicative criticism—that is, a difficulty in the relation between value and neutrality. It is a difficulty which arises with peculiar force from a proposition very clearly enunciated in our day—if not often very perfectly illustrated—the proposition that the critic's job is never to judge a poem (never, that is, to use either valuative or hortatory terms), but only to place the poem in its historical context and to elucidate, to compare, and to analyze. Thus Mr. Richards in one of his later statements, the "Introductory" to his *Practical Criticism* (altering his earlier view):

There is, it is true, a valuation side to criticism. When we have solved, completely, the communication problem, when we have got, perfectly, the experience, *the mental condition* relevant to the poem, we have still to judge it, still to decide upon its worth. But the later question nearly always settles itself; or rather, our own inmost nature and the nature of the world in which we live decide it for us.[14]

And Mr. Eliot in several of his essays:

Comparison and analysis . . . are the chief tools of the critic. . . . any book, any essay, any note in *Notes and Queries,* which produces a fact even of the lowest order about a work of art is a better piece of work than nine-tenths of the most pretentious critical journalism . . . *fact* cannot corrupt taste.[15]

In the dogmatic or lazy mind comparison is supplied by judgment, analysis replaced by appreciation. Judgment

[14] *Practical Criticism,* New York, 1935, p. 11.
[15] "The Function of Criticism," in *Selected Essays,* New York, 1932, p. 21.

and appreciation are merely tolerable avocations, no part of the critic's serious business.[16]

The critic must not coerce, and he must not make judgments of worse or better. He must simply elucidate: the reader will form the correct judgment for himself.[17]

Mr. Eliot was presumably not thinking about the cosmic aspects of such statements, but the other terminus of the scale of thought intimated in his simple defense of *Notes and Queries* might be illustrated in this passage from Plotinus: "In the single system of Intelligence are embraced as in an envelope other envelopes within, other systems and powers and intuitions: it may be analysed not by a straight severance, but by progressive explication of the implicit." [18] That is to say, values are continuous with and embodied in experience, in the facts and the structure of the facts. You do not stick them in or add them on, as in a mere psychology of values. Furthermore, since value is an indefinitely flexible and analogical concept, coextensive with form and being, a something which is always different yet always the same—there is no excuse for intruding special terms of appreciation and evaluation into our elucidative criticism. Value is always implicit and indefinable. It looks after itself. "Beauty Looks After Herself." Criticism is the "progressive explication of the implicit."

Those seem to me to be the full entailments of the

[16] "Studies in Contemporary Criticism," *The Egoist,* V (October, 1918), 113. See Victor Brombert, *The Criticism of T. S. Eliot,* New Haven, 1949, pp. 9–10.
[17] "The Perfect Critic," *The Sacred Wood,* New York, 1930, p. 11.
[18] Quoted in E. R. Dodds, *Select Passages Illustrating Neoplatonism,* London, 1923, p. 46.

holistic and elucidative position. And how often have we all been tempted to pursue just that policy—prune away the terms of warmth, of pleasure, of admiration (our subjective impertinences), cut close to the contour of fact in a neutral and only implicitly critical style? How often has Mr. Eliot himself, perhaps, tried to do that? How often, however, have any of us succeeded?

If you look at *Catiline*—that dreary Pyrrhic victory of tragedy—you find two passages to be successful: Act II, sc. i, the dialogue of the political ladies, and the Prologue of Sylla's ghost. These two passages are genial. The soliloquy of the ghost is a characteristic Jonson success in content and versification. . . . This is the learned, but also the creative Jonson. Without concerning himself with the character of Sylla, and in lines of invective, Jonson makes Sylla's ghost, while the words are spoken, a living and terrible force. The words fall with as determined beat as if they were the will of the morose Dictator himself. . . . What Jonson has done here is not merely a fine speech. It is the careful, precise filling in of a strong and simple outline.[19]

This passage, so bristly with several kinds of evaluative terms, was not unfairly chosen. So far have the more influential critics of our time been from practicing a style of neutral explication (and I think here not only of Mr. Eliot but also especially of Mr. Leavis) that it would be nearer the truth to say that they have mainly depended on two nonexplicative powers: a confident good taste in the use of indexical signs (that is, pointing out passages and quoting them) and an ener-

[19] "Ben Jonson," *Selected Essays,* p. 130.

getic, authoritarian choice of evaluative and hortatory
signs—that is, telling us we ought to admire these passages. I for one am prepared to defend this use of critical instruments,[20] or at any rate to argue that the greatest influence of the critic is often exercised that way.
Was it not, for instance, the most conspicuous technique employed by Matthew Arnold? But at the moment I am more concerned to describe and justify the
kind of middle style of evaluative explication which
is illustrated to some extent in the passage from Eliot
just quoted and which has, of course, been the style
set for illustration in this conference. Incidentally, it
has also been demonstrated in Mr. Fergusson's paper
on *Macbeth* and Mr. Brower's discussion of a passage
in *The Tempest*.

Our critical vocabulary, I venture, may be divided
roughly into three classes of terms: at one extreme the
terms of most general positive and negative valuing
(of which "good poem" or "excellent poem" may be
taken as the center and type), at the other extreme
the numerous neutral or nearly neutral terms of more
or less technical description ("verse," "rhyme," "spon-
dee," "drama," "narrative") and going with these in
degree of neutrality the whole vocabulary of referen-

[20] "Some of the most shining passages are distinguished by comma's
in the margin: and where the beauty lay not in particulars but in
the whole, a star is prefixed to the scene. This seems to me a shorter
and less ostentatious method of performing the better half of Criticism (namely the pointing out an Author's excellencies) than to
fill a whole paper with citations of fine passages, with *general ap-
plauses,* or *empty exclamations* at the tail of them." (Alexander Pope,
"Preface to Shakespeare," in his *Works,* ed. by Warburton, 1751, VI,
415.)

tial content ("love," "war," "life," and "death")—and
between those extremes the numerous and varied
terms of special valuation—"dreary," "determined,"
"careful," "precise," "strong," "simple"—terms which
of course assume their character of positive or negative valuing partly from the complex of more neutral
terms among which they are set and partly from the
flow of valuing started by more general and explicit
terms—"success," "successful," "genial," "creative."

It is true that the history of literary criticism shows
a more or less constant regression of key value terms
toward the level of neutrality—a movement of value
predicates into neutral subject positions—as the
growth of poetic styles and the appearance of inferior repetitions, or the maneuvers of critical dialec-
tic itself, the assaults and counterassaults of theory,
compel finer and finer discriminations. Croce has
commented amusingly on the utility of such terms as
"realistic" and "symbolic," "classic" and "romantic"
for either positive or negative valuing.[21] We have
heard of "true wit" and "false wit" (even "mixed
wit"), of "fruitful" and "unfruitful" ambiguities. This
protean character of our valuative terminology is a
function of the analogical and indefinable character of the poetic, the individual concreteness which
in each different poem is strictly relevant to the requirements of the poetic formula.[22] The *je-ne-sais-*

[21] J. W. Bray's neglected book *A History of Critical Terms* (Boston,
1898) is a good anthology of English critical terms in their contexts,
with a suggestive Introduction.
[22] There have been various ways of stating the principle: as that a
poem is individual as well as universal, that it is a Kantian "example

quoi or magic of the poem, we understand, is not a mere finishing touch, a stroke or note added here or there, but the form itself, in which the material and neutral elements transcend neutrality and are poetic. The reasons for approval and disapproval given in our criticism are never literally universal reasons, but must always be taken in the light of the example we are talking about. When Pope in his *Peri Bathous* (ch. x) gives the mock rule "Whenever you start a Metaphor, you must be sure to run it down, and pursue it as far as it can go," there can be no doubt that he puts his finger on the folly of the passages which he quotes from Blackmore's *Job* and *Isaiah*. Yet the same formula of consistency in the working out of metaphors is that by which critics of our generation have praised metaphysical poetry and by which one critic has even found the measure for patronizing the sonnets of Shakespeare.

Another way of stating what this means for critical terminology is to say that the terms at the bottom of the critical scale, the merely neutral, can never add up to a demonstration of the top term, "excellent poem." [23] That is, no definition of "excellent poem" has ever been achieved in a merely neutral, scientifically measurable predicate. Value is not translatable

---

of a rule which we cannot state," that there are graces beyond the reach of art or ineffable extras, that rules cannot make an artist, that no critical formula can work by itself, mechanically, without a critic inside it. "Could a rule be given from *without*," says Coleridge, "poetry would cease to be poetry, and sink into a mechanical art" (*Biographia Literaria*, ed. by Shawcross, II, 65).

[23] "With nothing can we touch a work of art so little as with critical words." R. M. Rilke, *Letters to a Young Poet*, trans. by M. D. Herder Norton, New York, 1934, p. 15.

into neutrality. If value is in the whole, then analysis must tend toward neutrality.

Nevertheless, our intuition of any complex whole will be improved by analysis. The effort of critical analysis and of explication is inevitably an effort to bring the two extremes of the critical scale together, the means or boosters toward this end being the intermediate terms of value—those of luster or dullness, warmth or chill, speed or slowness, and the like as such opposites happen to be appropriate to our criticism, and in all the variety of ways in which they can fit the contours of the poem—parts as well as whole—and interpret the parts in the direction of total value. Such value terms may be subdued; they may rely very little, if at all, on pointing by explicit and general value terms. It is, perhaps, under these conditions that they are most serviceable—that is, when they add to a strongly concrete and determinate coloration merely the accent of value.

It is easy to imagine instances, and to cite them from our scholarly literature, of simply neutral, philological, or otherwise historical explanation—where "explication" means glossing, that is, going outside the poem to understand its references, or where this shades into telling the content of the poem. ("This poem alludes to a society prank and tiff in the time of Queen Anne; it deals with the vanity, of beaux and belles, with courtship and maidenly resistance.") It is also possible to conceive adding to such description certain simply technical notes—concerning, for instance, burlesque narrative or heroic couplets. It is further possible to conceive and cite instances wherein these types of neutral explication are enhanced by the addition of some general value term, such as "successful," "aesthetically satisfying," or "brilliant," but nothing has been done to bridge the gap between the neutral explicative materials and the value term or to establish the right of the former to a wedding with the latter. But, finally, it is possible to conceive and to cite instances in which explication in the neutral senses is so integrated with special and local value intimations that it rises from neutrality gradually and convincingly to the point of total judgment. It is important to observe that in such instances the process of explication tends very strongly to be not merely the explication of the explicit but also the explicitation of the implicit or the interpretation of the structural and formal, the truth of the poem under its aspect of coherence.

The problem of explication which we have been examining is one which puts before us in a very compelling way both the desirability and the difficulty of finding an escape from the two extremes of sheer affectivism and of sheer scientific neutralism. I can make that point clearer by continuing the quotation from Mr. Eliot's passage about the laziness of the critic who judges. Mr. Eliot went on to say: "If the critic has performed his laboratory work well, his understanding will be evidence of appreciation; but his work is by the intelligence, not the emotions. . . . Where he judges or appreciates he simply . . . is missing out a link in the exposition." [24] But on these terms it scarcely makes much difference to rational criticism which side we take—whether we say the critic should judge or that he should not. One of the latest warnings against the use of judgment in criticism has been sounded by Professor George Boas in his *Wingless Pegasus; a Handbook for Critics.* And a reviewer in the *Times Literary Supplement* takes issue with him as follows: "This attempt would lead to the dehumanization of the whole relationship between the beholder and the work of art. Criticism has, inevitably, as much concern with the emotions as with logic." [25] That is, both Eliot and the *T.L.S.* reviewer (though on opposite sides of the argument) put judgment and appreciation in the area of emotion; criticism in a separated area of intelligence. And that is just what Mr. Richards did in his chapter on "Badness in Poetry," except that instead of "criticism" or "intelligence" he spoke of "communication." And later he said, in the passage I have quoted, that "communication" is the only thing with which the critic can deal. The extreme theory of explicative criticism cuts apart understanding and value just as much as does the avowed theory of affects— and that is another way of saying that our main critical problem is always how to unify understanding and value as much as possible, or how to make our understanding evaluative.

[24] "Studies in Contemporary Criticism," *The Egoist,* V (October, 1918), 113.
[25] *T.L.S.,* April 20, 1951, p. 242.

At higher levels of abstraction certain middle terms by which poetry has been defined have tended to lose all neutrality and become value predicates nearly, if not quite, synonymous with the subject "good poetry" or "excellent poetry." Yet it may be that the best of these terms, those which define poetry as a kind of order and wholeness, are able to preserve on one side their character of the analyzable while on the other taking on the indefinable and unanalyzable meaning of "poetry." For these are terms which point toward the intelligible and perspicuous (toward the implicit which may be explicated) rather than toward the opaqueness of the merely individual, concrete, or vivid. Terms of form and order keep to the public object and enable a critic to make more and more relevant observations about any specific work. And translated into a statement about theory, this is to say that formal and intellectual theory is theory *par excellence*. It is what is implied in the very concept of a theory—if, that is, there is to be any correspondence between the form of our thoughts and their content—more simply, if we are to know what we are talking about.

Idiom of Popular Poetry in the
Miller's Tale

🌺

By E. T. DONALDSON

A POET WHO ABANDONS the poetic idiom of his time and nation and devises one entirely new in its place creates for the would-be critic of his language a difficult problem. Criticism of the language of poetry can exist only through comparison with contemporary and earlier writings, and when, as sometimes happens, the critic cannot find between these and the work of the innovator enough similarity even to reflect the differences, he has to resort, in lieu of criticism, to merely quoting the innovator admiringly. With Chaucer the problem is even greater than with Milton, Shakespeare, Wordsworth, or Eliot. For while we may at least be sure that they were brought up in an English literary tradition from which they more or less consciously revolted, the disquieting suspicion always arises that Chaucer, bred if not born in a culture predominantly continental, may not have been very much aware of the literary tradition from which he was presumably in revolt; and this means that anyone who, in search of comparisons with Chaucer's diction, goes to the most prolific of the vernacular literary traditions, the romance, or to the closely related lyric, must consider himself to be in danger of wasting his time.[1]

But Chaucer did, after all, write in English, however continental his background may have been, and it stands to reason that diligent search will reveal at least a few correspondences with the popular English poetic diction of his day. Complete analysis of his own vocabulary is now—and has been for some time—possible through use of the Chaucer *Concordance;*[2] in this one can study all the contexts of every word he ever used, and hence can try to determine the values he placed upon the words he appropriated from the conventional vocabulary of popular poetry. It is the evaluation of these borrowings that I have undertaken; but since the job is a tricky one at best, I have thought it advisable to begin with those words which, while common in contemporary romance and lyric, occur only a very few times in Chaucer and are therefore to be suspected of carrying a rather special sort of weight. Only by such drastic limitation of the subject can it be treated at all in the time allotted.

In approaching the problem of evaluation there are two subordinate poems that I have found to be of some help. The first is Fragment A of the Middle Eng-

[1] The researches of Laura H. Loomis in recent years have, however, done much to justify such comparison by demonstrating Chaucer's familiarity with the native romance tradition. See "Chaucer and the Auchinleck MS. . . ," in *Essays and Studies in Honor of Carleton Brown*, New York, 1940, pp. 111–28; "Chaucer and the Breton Lays of the Auchinleck MS," *SP*, XXXVIII (1941), 14–33; and her study of "Sir Thopas" in *Sources and Analogues* . . . , Chicago, 1941, pp. 486–559.

[2] Ed. by Tatlock and Kennedy, Washington, 1927.

lish translation of the *Roman de la Rose*. That this is really Chaucer's work cannot be entirely proved. Most scholars think it is,[3] and I have little doubt that it is. But even if it is not, it is at least the sort of poem we should suppose him to have written in his poetic immaturity. For while it is not nearly so free as Chaucer's mature works are from that conventional diction— those clichés—by which the whole vernacular tradition was infected,[4] it nevertheless frequently has that quality, common to all Chaucer's indisputable works, of uniting perfectly simple English words with extraordinary ease into genuinely poetic language of a kind that makes the phrase "poetic diction" seem entirely too high-flown to be apt. Whether it is by Chaucer or not, its diction, occasionally but not consistently conventional, seems to represent a half-way point between popular English poetry and the *Canterbury Tales*. I find it critically illuminating, therefore, in comparing the Fragment with the *Canterbury Tales,* to observe how the mature Chaucer places in new and sometimes startling contexts words which a poet of somewhat less refined taste (probably the young Chaucer) had used flatly in time-honored contexts.

[3] For a summary of scholarly opinions on the authorship of the Fragment see Joseph Mersand, *Chaucer's Romance Vocabulary*, New York, 1939, p. 60, n. 7.

[4] See, for instance, the old poetic word "swire" (neck); and the conventional alliterative phrases *styf in stour* and *byrde in bour*. To conserve space, location of lines from Chaucer and the *Roman* will not be given: they may be readily found with the help of the *Concordance*. Quotations from Chaucer are from F. N. Robinson's edition, Boston, 1933.

Rather firmer help is offered by Chaucer's *Sir Thopas*. For this parody, while a criticism of vernacular conventions of every sort, is above all a criticism of standard English poetic diction. Therefore, if we find—as we do—words that Chaucer makes fun of in *Sir Thopas* showing up in seemingly innocent contexts elsewhere in his work, we shall have at least a small area in which to exercise criticism of Chaucer's idiom. Let me confess at once that the total critical yield from the words of this sort that I have noticed is not great and that it makes possible, not a wider appreciation of Chaucer's more serious poetry, but of some of his comic effects. In this paper I shall deal largely with the effect upon the *Miller's Tale* of certain words introduced from the vernacular poetic tradition. It goes almost without saying that this effect is ironical and that more irony is not the sole product I should have wished to achieve from my investigation. Still, this is only a beginning, and "after this I hope ther cometh moore"—if not from me, from better critics. The following is therefore presented as an example of a technique by which it may be possible to arrive at a better understanding of Chaucer's poetic idiom.

Since in the *Miller's Tale* I shall be dealing with ironical context, I shall start with an illustration of an ironical use of conventional idiom that is, thanks to the brilliant work of Professor Lowes, known to every Chaucerian. Lowes has demonstrated that the key to the portrait of the Prioress is in the second line, which, in describing her smiling as "ful symple and coy," endows her with a pair of qualities that were also those of innumerable heroines of Old French romance.[5] It is, incidentally, a measure of Chaucer's gallicization, as well as of his tact with a lady who likes to speak at least a sort of French, that these conventional words, along with most of the others in her characterization, are not commonly applied to ladies in Middle English romance. Furthermore, Lowes shows that in describing her person—gray eyes, delicate soft red mouth, fair forehead, nose *tretys*—Chaucer borrows from stock French descriptions of ladies details that were full of courtly reminiscences for the cultivated reader of the time, though with impeccable taste he foregoes the complete physical catalogue that an Old French heroine would feel herself entitled to. If Lowes had wished to reinforce his point, whose delicacy needs no reinforcement, he could have gone on to examine Chaucer's own works for the reappearance of the words used to describe the Prioress. He would have found, for instance, that "coy" is used of no other woman in Chaucer, though it appears in the stereotype "as coy as a maid," used only of men. "Simple," as Lowes does observe, is also the attribute of Blanche the Duchess —Chaucer's most serious conventional portrait; but it is applied further to three romantic ladies in the first fragment of the *Roman,* and, in Chaucer's mature work, it is used twice of Criseide, perhaps in a delicate attempt to be suggestive about her manner without being communicative about her character. It is worthy

[5] J. L. Lowes, "Simple and Coy . . . ," *Anglia,* XXXIII (1910), 440–51.

of note that the Prioress' nose *tretys* is foreshadowed by the face *tretys* of Lady Beauty in the English *Roman;* but the word is otherwise non-Chaucerian. Further, while ladies' noses receive full treatment in the translation of the *Roman,* elsewhere the only female nose mentioned is the stubby one that the miller's daughter inherited from her father in the *Reeve's Tale*—"With kamus nose, and eyen greye as glas," an interesting mutation, incidentally, on the Prioress, "Hir nose tretys, hir eyen greye as glas." And of all the women in Chaucer, only the Prioress and Alison, heroine of the *Miller's Tale,* have mouths or foreheads worthy of note: a case, perhaps, of the Colonel's Lady and Judy O'Grady. Finally, if one had time one might, I think, profitably investigate the words "fetys" and "fetisly," both used in describing the Prioress, but elsewhere appearing only in contexts which render highly suspect the particular sort of elegance they suggest.[6] In any case, the Prioress' portrait is a masterpiece of idiomatic irony, though the idiom is that of French poetry rather than of English.

With this much preliminary let us turn to the *Miller's Tale.* Upon this, Chaucer's worst ribaldry, it is generally agreed that he lavished his greatest skill, and in particular upon his description of the three principal characters—Alison, Absolon, and *hende* Nicholas, and upon their dialogue with one another. One of the devices he used most skillfully was that

[6] Aside from Fragment A of the *Roman,* where the words are common, they are normally used only by lower-class speakers; the only exceptions are in the portraits of the Prioress and the Merchant.

of sprinkling these characterizations and conversations with clichés borrowed from the vernacular versions of the code of courtly love—phrases of the sort we are accustomed to meet, on the one hand, in Middle English minstrel romances and, on the other, in secular lyrics such as those preserved in Harley MS 2253—but phrases that are not encountered elsewhere in the serious works of Geoffrey Chaucer. The comic effect of this imported courtly diction will, I hope, be understood as we go along. At the start it is necessary to bear in mind only that by the fourteenth century at least, the aim and end of courtly love was sexual consummation, however idealized it may have been made to appear, and that of the various factors upon which the *ars honeste amandi* depended for its idealization the conventional language associated with it was not the least important.

The key to the matter, as one might expect, is in the constant epithet applied to the hero of the *Miller's Tale*—that is, in hende Nicholas' almost inseparable *hende*. Any one who has done even cursory reading in popular English poetry of Chaucer's time—and before and after—will heartily agree with the *Oxford Dictionary's* statement that "hende" is "a conventional epithet of praise, very frequent in Middle English poetry." Originally it seems to have meant no more than "handy, at hand"; but it gradually extended its area of signification to include the ideas of "skillful, clever" and of "pleasant, courteous, gracious" (or "nice," as the *Oxford Dictionary* says with what I take to be exasperated quotation marks); and it simultaneously extended its area of reference to include, under the general sense "nice," almost every hero and heroine, as well as most of the rest of the characters siding with the angels, in Middle English popular poetry. Thus, the right of the Squire of Low Degree to the hand of the King's Daughter of Hungary is established by the minstrel poet's exclamation:

> The squir was curteous and hend,
> Ech man him loved and was his frend.

And another poet boasts of Sir Isumbras,

> Alle hym loffede, that hym seghe:
> Se hende a man was hee! [7]

Such examples could be multiplied indefinitely. Indeed, the average popular poet could no more do without "hende" than he could do without the lovers whose endless misadventures gave him his plots, since unless a lover was "hende," he or she was no proper exponent of courtly love. We should, therefore, have a right to expect the adjective to modify such Chaucerian characters as Troilus and Criseide, Arveragus and Dorigen, Palamon, Arcite, and Emily. But in Chaucer's indisputable works the word, while it is used eleven times with Nicholas, appears only twice elsewhere, and it is applied to none of the more serious characters, such as those just mentioned. The translator of Fragment A of the *Roman* had, to be sure, used it twice to describe

---

[7] *Squyr of Lowe Degre*, ed. by Mead, ll. 3–4; *Sir Ysumbras*, ed. by Schleich, ll. 17–18; for examples of many of the characteristics discussed here, see W. C. Curry, *The Middle English Ideal of Personal Beauty*, Baltimore, 1916.

amiable folk associated with the garden of the Rose; but thereafter it is spoken only by the Host, that distinguished exponent of bourgeois good manners, when he calls upon the Friar to be "hende" to the Summoner; and by Alice of Bath, who expresses with it the charm possessed by her fifth-husband-to-be, jolly Jankin, who is a spiritual sibling of Nicholas' if there ever was one. It is clear from these usages, as well as from the even more eloquent lack of its use in any genuinely courtly context, that for Chaucer "hende" had become so déclassé and shopworn as to be ineligible for employment in serious poetry.

But by the same token it was highly eligible for employment in the *Miller's Tale*. Nicholas is, after all, a hero of sorts, and he deserves to be as "hende" as any other self-respecting hero-lover. But in the present context the word mocks the broad meaning "nice" that is apparent in non-Chaucerian contexts. Indeed, its constant association with Nicholas encourages one to feel that here "hende" does not so much define Nicholas as he defines it. Furthermore, he defines it in a way that is surprisingly true to the less usual senses of the word, for Nicholas turns out to be a good deal less romantically "nice" than he is realistically "clever, skillful." He even represents the earliest meaning of the word, "at hand, handy"; for the Miller, analyzing his love-triangle in proverbial terms, remarks that always the "nye slye" (the sly dog at hand, Nicholas) displaces the "ferre leeve" (the distant charmer, Absolon). But most important, in Nicholas as in other heroes, the quality of being "hende" is the cause of his success in love. In the quotations given above we learn that it was because they were "hende" that Sir Isumbras and the Squire of Low Degree were generally beloved. Nicholas is also lovable, but his lovableness is of the rather special sort that would appeal to a woman of Alison's tastes and morals. In short, the coupling of word and character suggests in Nicholas nothing more than a large measure of physical charm that is skillful at recognizing its opportunities and putting itself to practical sexual use; and this is a sorry degradation for an adjective that had been accustomed to modify some of the nicest people in popular poetry, who now, as a result of Nicholas, begin to suffer from guilt by association.

A somewhat similar aspect of Nicholas' character is reflected in the line that tells us,

> Of deerne love he koude and of solas.

For his aptitude at *derne love*, "secret love," Nicholas must have been the envy of a good many young men in contemporary English poetry. For instance, in the Harley MS we meet several swains whose unsuccessful involvement in secret love affairs is their chief source of poetic woe.

> Lutel wot hit any mon
> hou derne loue may stonde,

grumbles one of these before going on to explain with what agonies and ecstasies it is attended.[8] Such lyricists

8 See *The Harley Lyrics,* ed. by G. L. Brook, University of Manchester, 1948, 32.1–2; also 3.36 and 9.43 (references are to poem and line numbers).

were probably apt to pretend to themselves that the secretive line of conduct suggested by the phrase "derne love," while it may have made things difficult, was nevertheless one of the ennobling conditions imposed upon them by the courtly code. Chaucer, however, seems to have felt otherwise, for while many of his heroes experience "secree love," none besides Nicholas is ever "derne" about it. Elsewhere Chaucer does not even use the common adjective to modify other nouns besides "love," apparently feeling that its reputation had been ruined by the company it had kept so long. Even in Old English, of course, the word was ambiguous, reflecting sometimes justified secrecy and sometimes secret sin; and among the moral lyrics of the Harley MS there is one whose author makes it clear that for him "derne dedes" are dirty deeds.[9] From his avoidance of the adjective it appears that Chaucer also subscribed to such an opinion. Moreover, the modern reader of the Harley love lyrics will probably sympathize with him, for it sometimes seems that, whatever the lovers pretended, they respected the principle of "derne love" more because of its value in protecting them from outraged husbands or fathers than from any courtly ideal of preserving their lady's good name.[10] Thus, long before Chaucer's time "derne love" was already in potentiality what it becomes in actuality in Nicholas, a device for getting away with adultery, if not really a sort of excuse for indulging in it. Therefore Nicholas' aptitude parodies an ideal already devalued through misuse in the vernacular;

[9] See *OED*, "dern," and Brook, 2.5–11.　　[10] See Brook, 24.17–20.

and since even at its most exalted the courtly code of secrecy might be described as crassly practical, his aptitude also parodies that of more genuinely courtly lovers than the Harley lyricists.

Turning to Nicholas' rival, jolly Absolon, one may find further instances of this technique of Chaucer's. What Absolon lacks in the way of Nicholas' "hende-ness" he tries to make up with his own "joly-ness." The epithet "joly" is not as consistently used with Absolon as "hende" is with Nicholas, and since it has a wide variety of meanings and is common in Chaucer, it may not be so readily classified. Suffice it to say that it is generally in the mouths of bourgeois characters and that in the senses "handsome" and "pretty" it modifies men or women with equal frequency. But it is, perhaps, the secret of Absolon's ill-success that all his jollification makes rather for prettiness than for masculine effectiveness. One recalls that Sir Thopas, though a sturdy hero, possesses some of the charms of a typical medieval heroine, and the Miller seems to suggest by several of the terms in his portrait of Absolon that the latter had somehow or other fallen across the fine line which in medieval poetry separated feminine beauty from that of beardless youths. For in his description he uses words that a minstrel poet would normally apply to a pretty girl. For instance,

> His rode was reed, his eyen greye as goos,

and the gray eyes will remind us of the Prioress, as well as of countless other medieval heroines and, it must be granted, a number of heroes, though not in

Chaucer, who reserves gray eyes for ladies. But in pos-
sessing a "rode"—that is, a peaches-and-cream complexion recommended by fourteenth-century Eliza-
beth Ardens, Absolon places himself in the almost
exclusive company of Middle English damsels.[11] The
complexion of truly manly males of the time was,
after all, generally obscured by a good deal of beard,
and hence apt to remain unsung. It is significant that
the only other "rode" in all Chaucer belongs to Sir
Thopas, a feminine feature that contrasts startingly
with the saffron beard of that curiously constituted
creature. Absolon further distinguishes himself (from
his sex, I fear) by being the only character in Chaucer
to be associated with the adjective "lovely," which
is applied to the looks he casts upon the ladies of the
parish and to no other thing Chaucerian, though to
hundreds of things, especially things feminine, in
popular poetry.[12]

Readers of the latter would naturally expect the
flesh of this pretty fellow to be

As whit as is the blosme upon the rys,

and it comes as a surprise that it is not Absolon's flesh,
but his surplice, that is described in these terms. But
the line, either in much the same form or, if one wants
pink flesh, with the variation "as reed as rose on ris,"

[11] For examples see Curry, pp. 92–94. In contexts not concerned with
romantic love or lovers this word, as well as others discussed here,
was commonly employed without regard to gender.
[12] For an example see Brook, 14.32. *OED*, "lovely," records the word
at *Anel* 142, but Skeat and Robinson read "lowly."

is one of the clichés found almost inevitably in descriptions of women.[13] For instance, the variant form is applied to Lady Beauty's flesh in the *Roman* fragment. But in what we are sure is Chaucer's work there is elsewhere no such phrase—indeed, there is elsewhere no such thing as a "ris," "spray," at all. When he quietly transfers the conventional descriptive phrase from the body to the clothing that covers it—in this case Absolon's surplice—Chaucer is, of course, creating the humor of surprise; but more important, the trick enables him to evoke for the reader the hackneyed context, with all its associations, in which the phrase usually appears, while at the same time the poet can make literal use of the phrase's meaning in his own more realistic description. There is an even more effective example of this economy in the portrait of Alison, to which I shall now turn.

The pretty heroine of the tale exemplifies most brilliantly Chaucer's reduction of the worn-out ideal, expressed by the worn-out phrase, to its lowest common denominator of sexuality.

> Fair was this yonge wyf, and therwithal
> As any wezele hir body gent and smal.

Now the weasel, as Lowes has observed,[14] is Chaucer's own fresh image, and its effectiveness is obvious. But the fact that Alison's body is "gent and smal"—shapely and delicate—makes her the sister of every contemporary vernacular heroine who is worthy of having

13 Curry, p. 94; also Brook. 3.11, 5.32.
14 *Geoffrey Chaucer*, Oxford, 1934, p. 177.

a lover.[15] Lady Beauty, paragon of embraceable women in the *Roman,* is in a similar way shapely—

> Gente, and in hir myddill small—

and it is natural that Sir Thopas should be "fair and gent." Possibly with Sir Thopas "gent" has its non-physical sense of "high-born, noble," but in view of the fact that the poet later commends his "sydes smale" —an item of female beauty—one may detect in the word at least a suggestion of ambiguity. On the other hand, while many lovely women in Chaucer's known works are "gentil," none besides Alison is "gent." His third and last use of the adjective is in the *Parliament of Fowls,* where it describes, appropriately enough, the "facounde gent," the "noble" eloquence, of the down-to-earth goose (a sort of female Miller in feathers) who speaks so uncourtly of the tercel eagles' love dilemma. Thus, in applying the stale adjective "gent" to Alison's body the Miller seems to be regarding her from a point of view less ideal and esthetic than realistic and pragmatic.

As in the case of the Prioress, Chaucer's restraint (I suspect that here it is only a teasing sort of restraint) prevents him from listing—except for one startling detail—the other conventional charms of Alison's body. We might expect from the Miller that our heroine would be—as Lowes has said—"anatomized in good set similes as inescapable as death," as, for instance, is Annot of the Harley lyric "Annot and John." [16] But the reader who wants this is doomed to

15 Curry, p. 102.
16 See Lowes, *Geoffrey Chaucer, loc. cit.;* Brook, 3.11–20.

disappointment, for what he gets is less of Alison's body than of her wardrobe. Several of the conventional terms, however, that one expects to meet in corporeal catalogues are still present, even though they are applied only to her clothing. Her sides, to be sure, are not like the Harley Fair Maid of Ribblesdale's,

> Whittore then the moren-mylk,[17]

but her apron is, a quality it shares in Chaucer only with the silk purse of the pink-and-white fleshed Franklin. This same apron lies, moreover,

> Upon hir lendes, ful of many a goore.

Now "gore," which meant originally a triangular piece of land and later (as here) a triangular strip of cloth, hence by synecdoche a skirt or apron, is obviously a technical word, and the fact that Chaucer used it only twice may not be significant. But when one recalls the number of vernacular ladies—including Alison's namesake in the Harley lyrics—who were "geynest vnder gore," or "glad vnder gore," [18] one may, perhaps, become suspicious. To be sure, scholars assure us that these phrases, along with such variants as "worthy under wede," "lovesome under line," "semely under serk," are merely stereotyped superlatives and presumably have no sexual connotation.[19] But in their literal meanings they could have such a connotation, and in their origin they probably did have. For instance, the poet of *Gawain and the Green Knight*

---

[17] Brook, 7.77; also Curry, p. 81. [18] Brook, 4.37, 3.16.
[19] See *OED*, "gore," sb. 2, 2; *Sir Gawain and the Green Knight*, ed. by Tolkien and Gordon, rev. ed., Oxford, 1930, note on l. 1814.

speaks of the lady of the castle as "lufsum vnder lyne"
only when Gawain is being subjected by her to the
most powerful sexual temptation. And inasmuch as
Chaucer, violating his self-imposed restraint, takes
pains to mention the "lendes" (the loins), a word that
appears a little later in a frankly sexual context [20]—
that are hidden beneath the "gores" of Alison's apron,
it is possible that his employment of the word "gore"
is evocative as well as technical; that he is, indeed, by
providing a sort of realistic paraphrase of the conventional expression, insinuating what the lover of the
Harley Alison really had in mind when he called his
mistress "geynest vnder gore." This is only a possibility, and I should not want to insist upon it. But the
possibility becomes stronger when we recall Chaucer's
other use of the word [21]—in Sir Thopas' dream,

> An elf-queene shal my lemman be
> And slepe under my goore.

Whatever "gore" means here—presumably cloak—its
context is unmistakable.

Nowhere does Chaucer's idiom devaluate with
more devastating effect the conventional ideal to the
level of flat reality than in two sentences occurring
near the end of Alison's portrait. Like many a lyric
and romance poet the Miller discovers that he is not
clever enough to describe the total effect his lady produces—indeed, he doubts that any one is clever

[20] "And (Nicholas) thakked hire aboute the lendes weel."
[21] In MS Harley 7334, A3322 reads: "Schapen with goores in the newe
get," which Tatlock regarded as a possible Chaucerian revision: see
Robinson's textual note on the line.

enough. The poet of the *Life of Ipomedon* was later to remark of a lady,

> In all this world is non so wyse
> That hir goodnesse kan devyse,

while the Harley Alison's lover had already asserted,

> In world nis non so wyter mon
> That al hire bounte telle con.[22]

True to the convention, the Miller exclaims of his Alison,

> In al this world, to seken up and doun,
> There nys no man so wys that koude thenche
> So gay a popelote, or swich a wenche.

But the Miller's mind is not on the "bounte" (excellence) or "goodnesse" of Alison; and his crashing anticlimax, ending with the word "wenche," which, in Chaucer, when it does not mean servant-girl means a slut,[23] is a triumph of the whole process we have been examining. Another occurs a little later. Once more the Miller is following convention, this time comparing Alison to a flower. John had said of Annot in the Harley lyric,

> The primerole he passeth, the peruenke of pris,[24]

---

22 *Lyfe of Ipomydon*, ed. Koelbing, ll. 123–24; Brook, 4.26–27.
23 In his thorough study of the dialect of the *Reeve's Tale* in *Transactions of the Philological Society* (London) for 1934, p. 52, Tolkien observes that "wench" "was still a respectable and literary word for 'girl' in Chaucer's time, and was probably in pretty general use all over the country." But it was not a respectable word in Chaucer's eyes (except in the sense "servant-girl"), as a study of his uses will quickly reveal; see the Manciple's definition, H211–22.
24 Brook, 3.13; cf. 14.51–53.

and the Miller also begins his comparison with the cowslip, the "primerole":

> She was a prymerole, a piggesnye.

But the accompanying item is no longer a "pervenke of pris," an excellent periwinkle, but a "piggesneye," something which, while it may be also a flower (perhaps, appropriately enough, a cuckoo flower),[25] remains, unmistakably, a pig's eye. Beneath the Miller's remorseless criticism the Blanchefleurs and even the Emilys of Middle English romance degenerate into the complacent targets of a lewd whistle.

In their conversation with Alison the two clerks talk like a couple of Harley lyricists.[26] But Absolon, fated to accomplish more words than deeds, naturally has the richer opportunity to speak in the vernacular of love—or rather, to quote Absolon, of love-longing.

> Ywis, lemman, I have swich love-longynge,
> That lik a turtel trewe is my moornynge,

[25] See Manly's note, citing an *EDD* definition for Essex, in his edition of *CT*, New York, 1928, p. 560.

[26] One is frequently tempted to suggest that Chaucer had the Harley lyrics in mind when he was composing *MT*, but in view of the poor conditions that existed for the preservation of secular lyrics, to associate Chaucer with a few survivals seems too large an economy. Particularly close correspondences may be noted with the lyric "De Clerico et Puella" (Brook, 24), a dramatic dialogue in which a maiden initially repulses a clerk's plea of secret love: notice especially the third stanza, where she rebukes him ("Do wey, thou clerc, thou art a fol") and warns him of the consequences if he should be caught in her bower, and compare Alison's initial resistance ("Do wey youre handes") and her warning (A3294–7); further, the Harley lyric's window where the two had kissed "fyfty sythe" (l. 23), and the carpenter's shot window. But the situation is, of course, a very old one (see *Dame Sirith*), and the Harley lyric may go back remotely to the same source from which Chaucer's immediate source stems.

he laments outside her window. Love-longing was, of course, a common complaint, positively epidemic in the Middle Ages, and most of Chaucer's lovers have at least occasional attacks of it. But as with certain modern diseases, its name seems to have varied with the social status of its victim, and in Chaucer only Absolon and Sir Thopas are afflicted with it under that name. They are therefore in a tradition that includes knights as illustrious as Sir Tristram, not to mention those rustics the Harley lovers,[27] but fails to include Aurelius, Arcite, Troilus, or even the less admirable Damian. The inference is that for Chaucer the phrase "love-longing" implied a desire of the flesh irreconcilable with courtly idealism, though fine for Absolon. Absolon is also following popular tradition when he introduces the figure of the legendarily amorous turtle-dove into his declaration: "like a turtle true is my mourning." Ordinarily, however, it is the lady who is the dove, a "trewe tortle in a tour"[28]—faithful and remote in her tower, but curiously inarticulate, considering that she is a dove and that doves are rarely silent. Thus, the conventional image is reset in a context that is more natural and in this case more genuinely poetic. Another simile of Absolon's for conveying his distress—

I moorne as dooth a lamb after the tete—

is the Miller's own audacious contribution to the language of love, and demonstrates the ease with which

[27] See Brook, 4.5; *Sir Tristrem,* ed. by Koelbing, l. 1860.
[28] Brook, 3.22; cf. 9.3.

Chaucer, employing a sort of merciless logic, can move from a wholly conventional image involving animals to one wholly original and wholly devastating.

Elsewhere, Absolon keeps closer to what we should expect. Alison, for instance, is his "swete brĭd" or "brīd"—that is, his sweet bird, bride, or possibly even "burd" (maiden): as in the romances and love lyrics it is often difficult to tell which of the three the lover means, or whether he is himself altogether sure.[29] In the other works of Chaucer birds are clearly birds, brides clearly brides, and "burd" does not occur except once of a lady in the *Roman*. Perhaps, however, it is only fair to observe that Chaucer's avoidance elsewhere of this trite form of endearment results in a use of "dear heart" and of the substantive "swete" so excessive as to amount to a triteness of Chaucer's own devising.

Continuing in the lyrical tradition even after the shame of his débacle, Absolon calls Alison his "deerelyng"—the only instance in Chaucer of this indestructible term.[30] But Absolon's lyricism reaches its highest point, naturally, before his disillusionment when, close to what he mistakes for the Promised Land—in this case the shot-window of the carpenter's bower—he begs for Alison's favors—that is, for her "ore" (mercy), as lyric poets usually expressed it. A Harley poet de-

[29] The Harley lyrics have "burde," maiden (Brook, 3.1, 5.36), "brudes," maidens (6.39), "brid," maiden? (14.17), and "brid," bird for maiden (6.40). In the *King's Quair*, stanza 65, "bridis" rhymes with "bydis" (abides), but clearly means "birds."

[30] See, for instance, *William of Palerne*, ed. by Skeat, l. 1538.

scribing a similar crisis in his relations with his mistress reports,

> Adoun y fel to hire anon
> Ant cri[d]e, "Ledy, thyn ore!" [31]

And much earlier, according to Giraldus Cambrensis, a priest of Worcestershire had so far forgotten himself at the altar as to displace the liturgical response "Dominus vobiscum" with the lyrical refrain "Swete lamman, dhin are." [32] Thus, Absolon was conforming to a very old tradition when, about to receive his kiss, he

> doun sette hym on his knees,
> And seyde, "I am a lord at alle degrees;
> For after this I hope ther cometh moore:
> Lemman, thy grace, and sweete bryd, thyn oore!"

"Ore," the venerable word that is so often in the mouths of love-sick swains in Middle English, occurs in Chaucer only here. And the immediate similarity but impending difference between Absolon's situation and the situation of the average lyric lover epitomizes the technique we have been examining.

One final illustration of Chaucer's use—or abuse—of conventional idiom will suffice. Every reader of medieval romance knows that sooner or later the poet is going to describe a feast, if not a literal feast of food, at least a metaphorical one of love; and readers of English romances, including, in this case, Chaucer's own, can anticipate with some accuracy the terms in which

[31] Brook, 32.16–17.
[32] *Opera*, ed. by J. S. Brewer, II (London, 1862), 120.

the feast is going to be described—all the mirth and minstrelsy, or mirth and solace, or bliss and solace, or bliss and revelry, or revelry and melody by which the occasion will be distinguished. In the *Miller's Tale* the feast is, of course, of the metaphorical kind, consisting in the consummation of an adulterous love; and the obscene Miller, with his vast talent for realism, adapts the hackneyed old phrases most aptly to the situation. The carpenter, snug if uncomfortable in his kneading trough on high, is alternating groans with snores—"for his head mislay"—while Alison and Nicholas are in his bed below.

> Ther was the revel and the melodye;
> And thus lith Alison and Nicholas
> In bisynesse of myrthe and of solas.

At this feast the carpenter's snores furnish the "melodye," while his wife and her lover experience the "solas"—that seemingly innocent word for delight which here receives the full force of Chaucer's genius for devaluation—the completion of a logical process that began when we first heard it said of "hende" Nicholas that

> Of deerne love he koude and of solas.

It is, of course, true that the idiom I have been examining is just what we should expect of the Miller's cultural background—and of that of his characters [33]

---

[33] According to L. A. Haselmayer, "The Portraits in Chaucer's Fabliaux," *RES*, XIV (1938), 310–14, conventionalized portraits existed —though in only a vestigial form—in the French fabliaux with which Chaucer was acquainted. It was perhaps from these that Chaucer got the idea of using conventional poetic idiom in ironic contexts.

—and it would be possible to dispose of it by simply labeling it "verisimilitude." But verisimilitude seems to me among the least important of artistic criteria, and I refuse to believe that the courtly idiom in the *Miller's Tale* accomplishes nothing more than that. Perhaps I should have made a larger effort than I have to distinguish the Miller from Chaucer, and my interchanging of their names must have grated on some ears. But as I see it, much of Chaucer's irony in the *Canterbury Tales* becomes operative in the no man's land that exists between the poet Chaucer—who if he read his poems aloud must have been a very personal fact to his own audience—and the assigned teller of the tale, whether the Miller, the Knight, or, in *Sir Thopas,* Chaucer the pilgrim. The irony produced by the use of popular poetic idiom in the *Miller's Tale* becomes operative in this no man's land and operates in several directions. First, the idiom tends to make of the tale a parody of the popular romance, rather like *Sir Thopas* in effect, though less exclusively literary. Then, too, it reinforces the connection between the *Miller's Tale* and the Knight's truly courtly romance that the *Miller's Tale* is intended to "quite" (to repay); for it emphasizes the parallelism between the two different, though somehow similar, love-rivalries, one involving two young knights in remote Athens, the other two young clerks in contemporary Oxford. And in so far as it does this, it tends to turn the tale into a parody of all courtly romance, the ideals of which are subjected to the harshly naturalistic criticism of the fabliau. But finally, while doing its bit in the accomplishment of these things, the idiom Chaucer borrows from popular poetry contributes to the directly humorous effect of the *Miller's Tale*, and that is probably its chief function.[34]

[34] Since this was written, Fr. Paul E. Beichner has in a delightful paper fully demonstrated the effeminacy of Absolon and its traditional nature; see "Absolon's Hair," *Mediaeval Studies*, XII (1950), 222-33.

Troilus and Cressida:
Music for the Play

※

By FREDERICK W. STERNFELD

O N AUGUST 3, 1952, the New York *Times* carried
the following notice:

> The effect of music on the individual and group be-
> havior . . . will be studied by . . . Teachers College,
> Columbia University, in co-operation with the Music Re-
> search Foundation and the New York City public schools.
> . . . An attempt will be made to determine . . . the ef-
> fects of music on human personality. . . . It has been
> known for many years that the influence of music on peo-
> ple is profound and greatly for the good. The question
> to be investigated is how music can best be used to pro-
> duce such effects with some degree of certainty.

To be sure, Shakespeare believed that the influence
of music on people was profound, although neither he
nor his Elizabethan contemporaries made any rash assumptions that this influence was always greatly to the
good. Nevertheless, the time span between this topical
announcement and the passages on music in Plato's
Republic offers us a perspective for an understanding
of Shakespeare's philosophy of music. The various
parts of that philosophy were a real force which determined the use of music in his plays and—as we shall

see—the belief in the power of music was one of the most important aspects of the Elizabethan creed. In his theater Shakespeare had at his beck and call a multitude of musical tools. But today these varied musical means of expression present challenging problems in the staging of the plays—problems which concern both the researcher who must unearth Elizabethan songs and dances and the modern composer who must provide his own settings when old ballads and airs are not available or acceptable. And, along with sound aesthetic judgment, an awareness of the Elizabethan beliefs about music must watch over these musical labors.

Two beliefs point clearly to the past. That is to say, they were as powerful in the Athens of Plato and Aristotle as in the last days of Roman civilization for Boethius; and from Boethius they were handed down through the Middle Ages up to and including the Renaissance. To these succeeding generations the concepts of the ethos of music (or the power of music) and of the music of the spheres were not dated superstitions, fit only for children and poets. One spelled good or evil; the other was as much a part of the heavens as the angelic host. But the generations after Shakespeare could only smile tolerantly at the scientific imperfections of a philosophy so admirable in other respects. It is true that the twentieth century has made an effort to reincorporate these beliefs into the modern picture of the world. Some of these endeavors are based on a modern mythology, derived from a new criticism and a new psychology; others on a modern physics, derived from new perceptions of a supersonic speed and infinite space; and still others on a modern medicine which has discovered new uses of therapeutic music. But these recent attempts to assimilate a discarded past are still tentative and far from being widely accepted. When, after the Second World War, a doctor extolled the therapeutic use of soothing music for shell-shocked veterans, his procedure was sanctioned by modern experiments and carried on according to the checks and proofs of modern therapy, which has very little regard for Plato, though it may be proud to quote him.

Similarly, we may clear our throats and tell our students that supersonic speed explains why the motions of the celestial orbs are not audible to the human ear. But that does not authenticate the music of the spheres to a youngster of our own age, though it may suggest that the old boys had some fuzzy notions that were not quite so crazy after all, though unnecessarily shrouded in baby talk and double talk. In other words, when we listen to Lorenzo's well-known strains from the *Merchant of Venice:*

> Look how the floor of heaven
> Is thick inlaid with patines of bright gold:
> There's not the smallest orb which thou behold'st
> But in his motion like an angel sings,
> Still quiring to the young-eyed cherubins;
> Such harmony is in immortal souls;
> But whilst this muddy vesture of decay
> Doth grossly close it in, we cannot hear it.

we must re-condition our minds to realize that Shakespeare is not indulging in poetic license, but is articulating a belief shared by the foremost humanists of the Renaissance, including professors of physics and of music. Of course, a footnote in small print may draw our attention to analogies with Kepler, Augustine, Boethius, or Plato, but such references are useless unless the reader recognizes in them a part of the intellectual Elizabethan climate, a climate which affected university wits and authors as well as the average spectator. In fact, the music of the spheres, and allied to it the music of the spirits and of the Aeolian harp, are indispensable parts of the philosophy behind several of Shakespeare's plays, such as *A Midsummer Night's Dream* and *The Tempest,* and echoes of it may still be found in Coleridge's "Aeolian Harp" and in the song of Ariel and his spirits in Goethe's *Faust.*

But our point of departure in this study is *Troilus,* a satirical tragedy, and as a work of this nature it is characteristically devoid of many references to the music of the macrocosm, since it is almost exclusively concerned with the foibles of the microcosm. Not that the projection from the individual microcosmic level to a more general plane is completely absent from *Troilus.* The passage from Ulysses' famous speech on degree

> Take but degree away, untune that string
> And hark what discord follows

clearly infers analogies between audible and inaudible music that are not mere metaphor and conceit, but buttressed by a firm philosophical tradition. Nevertheless, we should give our attention to the ethical concept of music, a belief whose recognition will aid our twofold purpose of understanding and staging the drama.

The belief in the ethos of music, or the ethical concept of music as it is also called, is derived from the Greek noun ἦθος (custom, habit, disposition), and although modern books written in English, French, and German dealing with the music of Greek antiquity, always discuss the concept, it has never been successfully translated into the vernacular. Let us, then, state briefly that the ethical concept of music implies that music affects the soul, the humor, the disposition of man, and that he who plays the right music at the right time will achieve the right effect. Fundamentally, this is a concept of primeval magic, reflected in the chants of the medicine man, as well as in Greek philosophy, where Dorian music makes man disciplined, martial, and courageous, while Ionian or Lydian music makes him soft, effeminate, and unfit for political or military discipline. This belief in the magical power of music, reflected in the myth of Orpheus, as well as in Plato's *Republic,* continued undiminished in vigor or importance, throughout the Christian era. Shakespeare articulates this attitude when he exclaims in *Measure for Measure* (IV, 1):

> . . . Music oft hath such a charm
> To make bad good, and good provoke to harm.

Now, theoretically the ethical concept establishes two kinds of music, one that helps church and state and one that weakens them. However, both in Plato's philosophy and in the Christian church the attendant censorship necessary to separate the sheep from the goats led to a general distrust of the art of music which was called "lascivious," "effeminate," "too artful," "too worldly," "popish," and by a variety of other labels, according to the prejudices of the censor. We have only to recall the famous section on the arts in Plato's *Republic* and, in the sixteenth century, the attitude of the Council of Trent toward church music, to realize that once you decree what is "good" and what is "bad," your zeal usually propels you to condemn more than half of the extant music.

The echoes of this attitude are to be found in the Calvinist opposition to pomp and circumstance and the disastrous effects it has had upon the music of Holland, Scotland, England, and New England. The point is that the Elizabethans associated with music the dangers to which a soft society was prone. The serious business of war and statesmanship were imperiled by irresponsible mirth and voluptuous euphony. This is, perhaps, nowhere clearer than in that moral and allegorical poem which deals with personified virtues and vices, the *Faerie Queene*. Both of the temptresses in the Second Book entice weak knights by an excess of music. The word "excess" must be stressed, for who could read Hoby's *Courtier* or Morley's *Introduction to Musicke* without realizing that some musical accomplishments were the expected part and parcel of a gentleman's background. But when these much-quoted passages are read in the context of Ascham's *Schoolmaster* and Elyot's *Governor,* we realize that music was part of a liberal education, but too much of it would mar a gentleman and might better be left to the loose and lesser folk, to professional musicians and entertainers. That is one of the reasons why, as a rule, the characters that sing in public in Shakespeare's plays are neither ladies nor gentlemen but their social inferiors. And when a gentleman does sing, as Balthasar in *Much Ado about Nothing,* the poet laboriously accounts for that exceptional performance. In *Hamlet* and *Lear* grave-diggers and clowns sing, but members of the nobility sing only when deranged or when simulating madness. Of course, Lord Pandarus sings in *Troilus*—in fact, he is the only character who does, but that is precisely what is rotten in the state of Troy, and we shall have more to say about this later. To return to the *Faerie Queene,* both Phedria and Acrasia weaken the manly resolutions of valiant knights by the excess of merriment and music. Of Phedria we are informed that

> Sometimes she sung as loud as lark in air
> Sometimes she laughed as merry as Pope Jone.

On her island there is

> No tree whose branches did not bravely spring
> No branch whereon a fine bird did not sit
> No bird but did her shrill notes sweetly sing
> No song but did contain a lovely ditt.
> Trees, branches, birds and songs were framèd fit
> For to allure frail mind to careless ease.

And when we learn of the temptation of Guyon, analogous to that of Cymocles, we learn that on the island the fields did laugh, the flowers freshly spring

> . . .
> And all the quire of birds did sweetly sing

> And told that garden's pleasure in their carolling
> And she more sweet than any bird on bough
> Would oftentimes amongst them bear a part
> And strive to pass (as she could well enough)
> Their native music by her skillful art:
> So did she all that might his constant heart
> Withdraw from thought of warlike enterprise.

Notice that here the temptress strives to surpass the natural music of the birds by her skillful and, we may add, sinful art. And in this very interplay of the natural and the lavish lies the beguiling seduction. When we behold Cymocles in the Bower of Bliss, we perceive "art striving to compare with nature." And seven cantos later Guyon, arriving at the same place, finds nature's work imitated by the "lavish affluence" of art.

The sumptuous pleasures of the Bower are three times listed in passages which employ the triple rhyme "joys-boys-toys," and the last of the three specifically enumerates music as one of the joys before giving an extensive description of the music itself. Guyon finds Acrasia's new lover

> In secret shade, after long wanton joys
> Whilst round about them pleasantly did sing
> Many fair ladies and lascivious boys
> That ever mixed their song with light licentious toys.

What song? we may ask. Just as Phedria had consorted her voice with the "quire of birds" in her garden, so now a solo voice sings a "lovely lay" which alternates with the music of the feathered kingdom.

> He ceased and then 'gan all the quire of birds
> Their diverse note t'attune unto his lay.

Parenthetically, the quire of birds chanting a lay which would seduce members of the gentry to stray from their proper course occurs in *2 Henry VI* [1, 3, 92] when Suffolk describes to the queen how he will induce proud Eleanor to betray her treasonable intentions.

> Madam, myself have limed a bush for her
> And placed a quire of such enticing birds
> That she will light to listen to the lays.

Spenser's Guyon is witness to a most intricate and therefore most seductive consort.

> Right hard it was for wight which it did hear,
> To read what manner music that mote be;
> For all that pleasing is to living ear
> Was there consorted in one harmony,
> Birds, voices, instruments, winds, waters, all agree:
>
> The joyous birds, shrouded in cheerful shade
> Their notes unto the voice attempered sweet;
> Th'angelical soft trembling voices made
> To th'instruments divine respondence meet;
> The silver sounding instruments did meet
> With the base murmur of the water's fall;
> The water's fall with difference discreet,
> Now soft, now loud unto the wind did call;
> The gentle, warbling wind low answerèd to all.

Now, what do we learn from Spenser's descriptions of music that debases man? For, clearly, all the examples quoted here "provoke harm," to use Shakespeare's phrase. And when Prynne, in *Histriomastix*, preaches that "lust-provoking Musicke is doubtlesse inexpedient and unlawfull unto Christians" [1] he re-

---

[1] G. H. Cowling, *Music on the Shakespearean Stage*, Cambridge, 1913, p. 3.

fers to the same interpretation of music within the ethical concept. What does it sound like? It is skillful, professional, sophisticated, striving to surpass—in its sensuousness—the beauty of natural music. Some of it is based on an interplay of voice and instrumental accompaniment; some of it is purely instrumental. In either case the instrumentation is affluent, lavish, colorful. Technically speaking, the consort is broken, that is, composed of different tone-colors. What in fairyland is a consort of birds, voices, instruments, waterfall, and wind, becomes in everyday Elizabethan practice the broken consort of, let us say, lute, guitars, viols, and wind instruments. Such a "broken" consort which employs different families of instruments is clearly more colorful and more exciting than a "whole" consort of viols, or a "whole" consort of recorders, or one of any kind restricted to a single family of instruments. An interesting corroboration of the preference for broken against whole consorts for entertainment is offered by the report of an English Jesuit College founded in 1592, which stressed particularly the study of music and of the theater. In enumerating and evaluating the various kinds of music, the whole consort of viols is termed "esteemed," but the broken consort "much more delightful for the reception of guests and persons of distinction." [2]

Spenser, in the *Faerie Queene,* Jonson in *The Poetaster,* and Shakespeare in *Troilus and Cressida* are all concerned with the English upper classes, with per-

[2] W. H. McCabe, "Music and Dance on a 17th-Century College Stage," *Musical Quarterly,* XXIV (July, 1938), 313–322 (particularly 314).

sons of distinction, and a fairly Italianate English gentry at that. What kind of music did their broken consorts play? What kind of song reflected the courtly, sophisticated atmosphere?

Let me first take up the purely instrumental music. The broken consort that issues from the festivities of Paris and Helen in Act III, Scene I, of *Troilus* is clearly music that provides an analogue to the old story of Nero's fiddling while Rome burns or to the music in Acrasia's Bower of Bliss. We must attempt to answer three questions: First, what instruments were being played? Second, what kind of music did they play? Third, what specific piece possesses the necessary quality of sensuousness?

The scoring called for in Morley's *Consort Lessons*, 1599, and in Rosseter's *Lessons for Consort,* 1609, offer practical cues for the instrumentation: treble lute, pandora and cittern (two kinds of guitars), bass viol, flute, and treble viol, would be a typical combination. In the absence of these ancient instruments we should not hesitate to use modern mandolins for lutes, guitars and banjos for pandora and cittern, and, if necessary, even a violin for a treble viol. The second question is one of repertory. What kind of music does a broken consort play? Generally speaking, fancies and dances. The contrapuntal fancy need not detain us here; simple dances—or groups of dances—are much more likely to fill the demands of stage music. Today we can either use pieces already scored for consorts or we can arrange a dance, written for a keyboard instrument, to any desired instrumental combination. The

Elizabethan repertory of virginal music was comparable in scope to the vast amount of piano arrangements current in the nineteenth century. Several large and important keyboard collections are extant and have been transcribed by nineteenth- and twentieth-century editors.[3] These collections have provided me with the piece I would choose for the broken consort in *Troilus.* For the third and ultimate question is never one of category, but one of individual choice. The piece must be a courtly dance, for although it does not actually function as dance music, it must serve as a stylized token of courtly dancing, as did so many compositions performed at real or at staged banquets or parties. While sophisticated and eligible for the merrymaking of the upper classes, it must at the same time be a distinctly popular number. I think the dance called "Mall Sims," arranged by Giles Farnaby in the Fitzwilliam Virginal Book, would fill our bill.[4] This piece, popular, courtly, and clever, was obviously much in

[3] *Fitzwilliam Virginal Book,* ed. by J. A. Fuller-Maitland and W. Barclay Squire, Leipzig, 1894–1899 (American reprints of the original German edition are available from Broude Bros., New York, and Edwards Bros., Ann Arbor, Mich.); *Mulliner Book,* ed. by Denis Stevens, London, 1951 (1st volume of a complete transcription, the collection contains sacred pieces for organ as well as secular dances); *Parthenia or the Maydenhead of the First Musicke That Ever Was Printed for Virginalls; Composed by William Byrd, Dr. John Bull and Orlando Gibbons,* ed. by J.H.A. & L. Farrenc, *Trésor des pianistes,* Paris, 1861–1872, Part VI (American reprint, with new introduction, Broude Bros., New York, 1951); *My Lady Nevell's booke,* ed. by H. A. Andrews, London, 1926 (particularly useful for military signals).

[4] William Chappell, *Popular Music of the Olden Times,* 2 vols., London, 1855–1859, I, 178. A more accurate version will be found in the *Fitzwilliam Virginal Book,* II, 447–448. Another arrangement may be found in the Lute Collection, *Sécret des Muses,* Amsterdam, 1615.

demand, for it appears in arrangements for the virginal and the lute, the favored instruments of the Italianate English gentry. The dance is also arranged for broken consort in both Morley's and Rossiter's *Consort Lessons*. The sophistication of the tune is obvious, I think, from the cleverness with which wide skips alternate with stepwise progressions. Moreover, its key of *d* minor and its skips of the minor sixth and scale runs frequently accompany descriptions of waste, profligacy, wantonness, and sensual excess in vocal music of the seventeenth and eighteenth centuries. This initial section, in slow notes, contrasts sharply with the quick notes of the middle section. The dance then concludes with a restatement of the stately beginning.

Another kind of instrumental music necessary in producing *Troilus* is indicated by such stage directions as "alarum," "retreat," "flourish," "tucket." These various ceremonious and military calls, which we might collectively summarize as "musical signals," are also descendants of the ethical concept of music. For the sound of wind instruments and drums which called man to battle was supposed to induce a war-like spirit, as was the martial rhythm in which these drum-rolls and brass fanfares were couched. However, while such connotations were not completely absent from the minds of Shakespeare's audience, they were of lesser importance. Alarums and flourishes functioned primarily as signals of communication which were supposed to convey to the characters on stage a call to combat and to the audience what was happening on the stage.

Shakespeare uses the term "alarum" more than seventy times as a stage direction.[5] In the vast majority of cases it means a drum signal to battle, just as the stage direction "retreat" means a drum signal calling off battle. But *Henry VI* and *Troilus* are exceptions to the rule, and in these two dramas trumpets are specifically indicated for alarums. In the former, Warwick challenges Clifford:

> And if thou dost not hide thee from the bear
> Now when the angry trumpet sounds alarum.

Similarly, in *Troilus* the stage direction reads "Alarum" before the fight between Ajax and Hector and "trumpets cease" after it. This raises the question of the meaning behind this exceptional use of trumpets in these two plays. Let me remind you first how analogous the two tragedies are in their intent to depict an arrogant and lavish society destroying itself in senseless war. Shakespeare is careful to establish the analogy when York's son (later Richard III) abuses the foreign queen in a ringing speech which clearly puts the blame for military and national disaster on her vicious influence.

> Helen of Greece was fairer far than thou
> Although thy husband may be Menelaus.

In other plays Shakespeare refers to Helen's beauty and the love she inspires, but in this instance he is interested in the social consequences. That the lesson of Troy was one to be learned by an Italianate English gentry is driven home when York's son proclaims

5 Edward W. Naylor, *Shakespeare and Music*, London, 1896, p. 165.

I'll play the orator as well as Nestor
Deceive more slyly than Ulysses could
And like a Sinon take another Troy

. . .

And set the murderous Machiavel to school.

What is the social meaning of trumpets? The instrument was among the carefully guarded privileges of the nobility, and only official court trumpeters were allowed to play it. The trumpeters belonged to a special guild and did not play in combination with other instruments. And in the language of military signals, drums referred to the infantry and trumpets to the cavalry. If we keep in mind that Shakespeare's Trojans and Englishmen fight the kind of war that was fought before cannons were used extensively, this means drums for the commoner and, again, trumpets for the nobleman. Moreover, in the ethical concept the trumpet has a definite effect upon live beings; it is supposed to excite not only valiant knights but their steeds as well. The unusual addition of trumpets, then, to the customary use of drums only for alarums in *Henry VI* and in *Troilus* suggests an aristocratic atmosphere of excessive sumptuousness, an extravagant society in real danger of self-destruction by exciting itself to senseless combat.

Ben Jonson, in *Cynthia's Revels,* carries this use of trumpets to denote a senseless and decadent excitement to absurd and ridiculous lengths. His bouts are not even real; rather, they are contests in the art of the courtier, depicting his skill in slick, sly, and smooth phrasing. Nevertheless, this mock tournament in courtship, in the most choice and cunning manner of addressing and complimenting a lady, is punctuated by no fewer than twenty trumpet signals. Devoid of their original meaning, they paint a devastating picture of the Italianate Elizabethan aristocracy.

The staging of *Troilus,* in addition to the use of drums for alarums and retreats and the use of trumpets and drums for the exceptional alarum opening the combat between Hector and Ajax, also calls for a "flourish" and "tucket." It does not prescribe the use of the sennet, a trumpet flourish somewhat longer than a tucket, since nowhere in the drama does Shakespeare require much time to fill or to clear the stage. Taking all of Shakespeare's plays together, the flourish occurs sixty-eight times as a stage direction; the sennet only nine times. Shakespeare apparently distinguished carefully between a short fanfare and a more elaborate brass piece for processional purposes, since in *Henry VI* the procession of the court to leave the stage is accompanied by the direction "Sennet. Flourish. Exeunt," that is, a sennet while they march off, and a flourish to signal the completion of the procedure. The tucket is a flourish which usually heralds the arrival of a particular person, such as Mountjoy in *Henry V* or Aeneas in *Troilus* when he conveys to the Greeks the challenge of Hector. Note that when Aeneas's arrival is announced the stage direction reads "Tucket," and in the following line Agamemnon asks, "What trumpet?" But some forty lines later, when Aeneas delivers the heart of his message, the actual challenge, he says:

> Trumpet blow loud,
> Send thy brass voice through all these lazy tents
> And every Greek of mettle, let him know
> What Troy means fairly, shall be spoke, aloud
>   [Stage direction:] "Sound trumpet"

Here Aeneas refers clearly to the ethical connotation of the trumpet sound, and the poet distinguishes between a general flourish and a specific tucket. The stage direction "tucket" occurs only seven times in all of Shakespeare's plays, and of these six connote foreigners rather than Englishmen. The exception is Goneril in *Lear*. Also, in all probability both the terms "sennet" and "tucket" are derived from the Italian, namely, from "sonare" and "sonata," on the one hand, and "toccare" and "toccata," on the other. However, these clues are more etymological than musical.

For alarums and retreats on the drums Naylor has provided a slow English and a quick French march.[6] These have not changed much through the centuries, and neither have the brass fanfares, whether they be performed on Renaissance trumpets, cornets, or modern bugles. Shakespeare's company probably used trumpets in the open-air public theater and the softer cornet in enclosed private theaters. As for the melodic line itself, it must be remembered that the Elizabethan trumpet did not possess a modern valve mechanism and was therefore largely restricted to the so-called natural notes or overtone series. For practical purposes, this means, that the motives are constructed largely of the three notes of the triad. And, indeed,

[6] *Op. cit.*, p. 209.

whenever trumpet signals occur in opera they usually are just simple triadic formulations up to the time of Beethoven's *Fidelio* and Wagner's *Tannhäuser* in the nineteenth century. It does not matter much, therefore, whether we take a historical flourish of Charles II's time, use Italian or French tuckets, or go to a much more recent source. In their simplicity these signals all sound very much alike and, indeed, as unequivocal symbols, modern audiences are much more likely to accept these fanfares than the songs and dances of the olden times whose styles have changed more profoundly in recent centuries.

Let me mention another Elizabethan source for drum and trumpet signals, a virginal piece by William Byrd known as "Mr. Bird's Battle." This composition is preserved in a MS at Christ Church as well as in "My Lady Nevell's Book," a virginal collection transcribed in 1926 by Hilda Andrews. The subtitles of various sections, such as "March of the Footmen," "March of the Horsemen," "Trumpets," "March to the Fight," and "Retreat," are obvious clues.

So far we have considered only instrumental music. And, indeed, most musical cues in *Troilus* are instrumental. But particular attention is due the songs of Pandarus, one complete in Act III, Scene 1, and fragments of another in Act IV, Scene 4. The three main types of vocal music widely known to Elizabethans and in current use for a diversity of secular purposes were the ballad, the air, and the madrigal. I have enumerated these three species in the order in which music asserts its importance and sometimes even its domination in these forms. They all represent a confluence and togetherness of poetry and music, but the relative contribution of the two components differs widely.

The Elizabethan air differs from the ballad much as the art song of the eighteenth and nineteenth centuries differs from folk song or popular ditties. The music is more important, more ambitious, more complex, and therefore more attractive to most composers of the age. The instrumental accompaniment is not some *um-ta-ta* which may be strummed when convenient or omitted when not. It is the indispensable part of an artistic dialogue, and such songs are usually performed by professionals or amateurs with exceptionally good training. The text is still easily understandable, each single syllable, word, phrase, both audible and intelligible, but a person with no musical background may have to strain a little so as not to miss the continuity of the words. And the words themselves, in their selection and in their prosody, will not be so simple and so expectable or (shall we say?) hackneyed—as those of the ballads. There will be a main rhythm, a main beat; but with more variation from the norm, and with more irregularity in the length of lines.

The madrigal, on the other hand, differs radically from ballad and air in that the music reigns supreme over the text. This is most obvious when it is performed by voices only, let us say, soprano, alto, 1st tenor, 2d tenor, bass. The contrapuntal interweaving of these voices, which sing the same syllables, words, and phrases, but not at the same time (except at the close) usually hinders an audience in understanding the text. Shakespeare uses the madrigal sparsely,[7] and, in fact, neither the madrigal nor the otherwise ubiquitous ballad [8] appear in *Troilus,* which is the subject of this study. The reason is clear enough, since Shakespeare was here concerned with aristocratic ways of music-making.

The air demands a trained singer, sometimes accompanied by other musicians, sometimes accompanying himself on the lute. It might be performed either by boy actors or adult actors, and whereas it is difficult to make a generalization not subject to exception it would seem that after the very early comedies Shakespeare made a clear distinction in the kind of songs he allotted to these two types. Of course, such a differentiation could apply only to male roles, since all female roles on Shakespeare's boards were acted by boys, and excellent singer-actors these boys must have been, judging from the songs allotted to Ophelia and Desdemona. But for male roles Shakespeare had a choice, and he seems to have favored adult actors for character songs and boy actors for magic songs. In magic songs we have another kind of music based on the ethical concept. Such music is sometimes instrumental, such as the harp playing of David, which consoled the sorrows of Saul, or the lyre-playing of Amphion, which charmed stones into forming the walls of the city of Thebes. Similarly, instrumental music

---

[7] Catherine Ing, *Elizabethan Lyrics,* London, 1951, p. 222.
[8] *English Institute Essays 1951,* New York, 1952, pp. 131 f.

helps restore Lear to sanity (Act IV, Scene 7) and spellbinds Leontes while the statue of Hermione comes to life (*Winter's Tale,* Act V, Scene 3). But frequently it is song which exercises the charm, and Orpheus of Greek mythology is, perhaps, the perfect example. In Shakespeare such songs are usually allotted to boys. Take, for instance, the three comedies in which the supernatural spirits are enacted by boys and which, in their fanciful make-believe, most closely approach the genre of the masque: *Midsummer Night's Dream, The Merry Wives of Windsor,* and *The Tempest.* The lullaby which the elves sing to charm Titania into sleep, "You spotted snakes with double-tongue," is closely related to the song with which fairies surround Falstaff at the conclusion of the *Merry Wives* to pinch, punish, and disillusion him and to create the merry confusion in which Fenton gains Ann Page. It has been convincingly suggested [9] that the model was provided by another Elizabethan magic song for boys, namely, in Lyly's *Endymion,* where a stage direction reads: "The fairies dance, and with a song pinch him, and he falleth asleep."

In the last plays Shakespeare returns once more to the musical skill of the boys and their magic, supernatural songs. "Come unto these yellow sands" is a veritable pied piper's lay, and the spell-bound Ferdinand must follow it into Prospero's realm, meditating as he goes that the power of Ariel's song was such that

> This music crept by me upon the waters
> Allaying both their fury, and my passion.

[9] Richmond Noble, *Shakespeare's Use of Song,* London, 1923, p. 60.

Of course, these three comedies were probably performed for special courtly occasions, and we may assume that Shakespeare had additional funds to hire extra boy singers. But even in the plays in which music is used sparingly, the magic songs are usually allotted to boys, as in *Caesar*, where Brutus asks that Lucius relieve his melancholy with his song; in *Antony*, where the Bacchanalian hymn, sung by a boy, adds its potency to the wine; and in *Measure for Measure*, where the boy sings for Mariana "Take O take those lips away," to please her woe, as she herself explains to the duke, who assures her that music oft hath such a charm to make bad good.

The clown Feste and his songs in *Twelfth Night* prove that Shakespeare's company also boasted a successful adult singer, probably William Kempe's successor, Robert Armin. It is difficult to believe that it was not he who sang the airs of Pandarus in *Troilus*. For these are not airs for which hired musicians are introduced, as in "Who Is Silvia?" or servants as in "Tell Me Where Is Fancy Bred." Nor are they magic songs, such as those of the elves or of Lucius. They are character songs, performed by one of the main protagonists of the drama, one whose importance transcends Balthasar in *Much Ado* or Amiens in *As You Like It* or even Feste. Shakespeare develops this species of air only gradually. In the early 1590's "Who Is Silvia?" and "Tell Me Where Is Fancy Bred" are given to adult characters, it is true, but not to one of the main actors and not to a nobleman. Both songs are expressive rather than magic: one expresses Thurio's wooing; the other Portia's advice to Bassanio, but they do not transport either Silvia or Bassanio into a different state of mind. There is, perhaps, a slight ethical connotation in Balthasar's song "Sigh No More, Ladies," in *Much Ado,* but together with the subsequent dialogue it really puts the idea of Beatrice's love into Benedick's mind more than that it charms him into being love-sick. After all, Benedick's first utterance after the song is "And he had been a dog that should have howled thus, they would have hanged him." But the important point about Balthasar's song is that for the first time Shakespeare has a nobleman sing an air. True, he is not one of the main characters, and he sings only reluctantly, deprecating his professional skill. But by these protestations the poet wishes to soften the social prejudices of his spectators and to prepare them for a dramatic innovation. Apparently the novelty was successful, for in *As You Like It* Amiens sings three airs, "Under the Greenwood Tree," "Blow, Blow Thou Winter Wind," and "What Shall He Have That Killed the Deer." Again we have the protestations expected of a nobleman. He complains that his voice is ragged after the first song, and Jaques has to goad him to the third, assuring him " 'tis no matter how it be in tune so it make noise enough." Again, the songs characterize the exiled duke and his court, the joys, hardships, and pastimes associated with the forest of Arden. On the other hand, the country wench Audrey and the plebeian clown Touchstone do not share the gentlefolk's melancholy infatuation with outdoor simplicity, and the song which presages their wedding is sung by two skilled singing boys in an elaborate fashion which smacks more of London than of the forest. Note that the two boy actors who perform "It Was a Lover and His Lass" poke fun at the way in which the gentry always protest too much before they sing:

First Page: Shall we clap into it roundly, without hawking or spitting, or saying we are hoarse, which are only the prologues to a bad voice?

Second Page: In faith, in faith, and both in a tune, like two gypsies on a horse.

Incidentally, here the song of the two boys is not a magic song, demonstrating that the division between character songs for adults and magic songs for boys is far from iron-clad. I think the introduction of the boys here is simply the result of the necessity of having trained vocalists for a duet, and different ones from Amiens at that.

Again, in *Twelfth Night* an adult singer performs the character songs. Contrary to Balthasar and Amiens, he is not a nobleman, but Feste, the clown, who characterizes either the jolliness of Sir Andrew in "O Mistress Mine" or the melancholy of the Duke Orsino in "Come Away, Come Away Death" or the general frolicking spirit when he concludes the comedy with "When That I Was a Tiny Little Boy." One of the reasons that Feste did all the singing may have been that neither the adult who played the duke nor the boy who played Viola possessed the necessary vocal skill. Some editors believe that Viola was supposed to have sung "Come away," but that the boy's voice cracked during an advanced stage of the rehearsals.

The noble Pandarus, like Balthasar and Amiens, is a lord and therefore reluctant to give, in public, a performance usually assigned to professionals. He protests to Paris that he is not full of harmony and to Helen that his art is rude, and he dallies some seventy lines before obliging with his song. But this courtly, sophisticated, self-indulgent, lecherous song characterizes the ills with which the Trojan gentry is infested as surely as Amiens paints the outdoor life of the Forest of Arden. No musical setting contemporary with Shakespeare has survived, and we must therefore find an Elizabethan air which fits the metrical requirements. A piece from a virginal collection transcribed by John Hawkins [10] provides us with music which suits the text surprisingly well. It adapts itself to the first half, which sets the mood, and also to the second, with its expressive music of words, for the "oh-ohs," "o-has," "ha-ha-hes," and "ha-ha-has" paint a corrupted sensuality almost by themselves.

This is certainly the perfect song of a pander, but beyond that Shakespeare establishes with elaborate care how aptly the song fits the Trojan and thereby the English aristocracy. The scene opens with the broken consort of music emanating from Priam's palace where Paris and Helen, the prototypes of depravity, are feasting. It is Paris who demands that

[10] New York Public Library, Drexel MS 5609, p. 143; reprinted in W. Chappell, *Popular Music of the Olden Time*, I, 202.

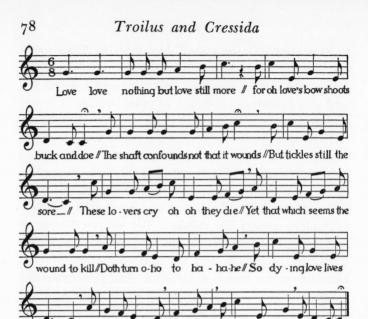

Love love nothing but love still more // for oh love's bow shoots buck and doe // The shaft confounds not that it wounds // But tickles still the sore __ // These lo-vers cry oh oh they die // Yet that which seems the wound to kill // Doth turn o-ho to ha-ha-he // So dy-ing love lives still __ // O-ho a while but ha-ha-ha // O-ho groans out for ha-ha-ha

Pandarus make up for the instrumental music he has interrupted by a performance of his own. When he praises him as "full of harmony" the term carries two meanings: first, the ability to perform music on a par with the complexity of a broken consort; this implies an air, since a ballad is primarily melody without harmony or with a negligibly simple harmony; second, Paris's praise implies that Pandarus possesses the skill to perform music as euphonius and voluptuous as the banquet music that he, Helen, and the courtiers have been enjoying. Helen, playfully, but also with the petulance of a lady who is accustomed to having her beauty win all arguments, persists in repeating Paris's

request against all protestations of Pandarus's modesty
and to the detriment of the business on hand, namely,
the message of Troilus which Pandarus wishes to convey to Paris. Finally, Helen prescribes the theme of the
lyric:

> Let thy song be love: this love will undo us all.
> Oh, Cupid, Cupid, Cupid

Paris confirms the theme and names the title of a
presumably well-known piece: "Ay, good now ['] love,
love, nothing but love [']."

And Pandarus finally obliges, accompanying himself
on the lute, the aristocratic instrument for the rendi-
tion of airs. That he is his own accompanist is made
clear from the dialogue, when he asks Helen: "Come,
give me an instrument, sweet Queen." The very ap-
pellation "sweet" used so excessively and effeminately
throughout the scene makes clear that Pandarus represents a stylization of the turn of mind which possesses
Paris, Helen, and other courtiers. Pandarus uses the
term fourteen times in the scene, sometimes singly,
such as "honey-sweet Queen," sometimes in groups of
three, such as "Sweet queen, sweet queen. That's a
sweet queen, in faith." But Helen, who calls Pandarus
"honey-sweet Lord" and "sweet Lord" and herself a
"sweet Lady" whom Pandarus must not make sour by
refusing to sing, clearly uses the same language as a
token of the same mind.

Sweetness as an indication of excessive softness is
also apparent in the "sweet music" in *Cynthia's Revels,*
by Jonson. Two of the courtiers are practicing the art

of courtship, the fashioning of a graceful phrase to compliment a lady. They exclaim: "All variety of divine pleasures, choice sports, sweet music, brave attire, soft beds, and silken thoughts attend this dear beauty." What makes this enumeration of divine pleasures particularly significant is that Jonson repeats it, in its entirety, four times within the scene. Thus, the ingredients with which he paints an atmosphere composed of sweet music, soft beds, and silken thoughts are carefully established, emphasized, and re-emphasized in the minds of his listeners. This soft sweetness in *Cynthia,* as well as in *Troilus,* is the same as in Spenser's Bower of Bliss, where "sweet words" drop like "honey-dew," just as Spenser's comparison of Cymocles with an "adder lurking in the weeds" parallels the "generation of vipers" in the dialogue following Pandarus's song. This dialogue also introduces another descriptive term with which Shakespeare characterizes the tempestuous sensuousness at the Trojan court—an adjective which distinctly adds to the suggestions of sweetness and softness in the analogous descriptions of Spenser and Jonson.

Helen: In love, in faith, to the very tip of the nose.
Paris: He eats nothing but doves, love; and that breeds hot blood, and hot blood begets hot thoughts, and hot thoughts beget hot deeds, and hot deeds is love!
Pandarus: Is this the generation of love? hot blood? hot thoughts and hot deeds? Why they are vipers: is love a generation of vipers?

And the lines immediately following make quite clear that the vipers who have tasted hot love and listened to hot music are neglecting their knightly duties, for we learn that this very day Helen has prevented Paris, and Cressida Troilus, from fighting in the field.

Pandarus's air, then, is the music of a depraved Elizabethan gentry, just as the broken consort which he interrupts. In his song several of the important aspects of Shakespeare's philosophy of music are fused. Quite properly he is reluctant to sing in the earlier part of the scene, and quite improperly does he sing later, for too much music mars manners and valor, and a gentleman who spends too much time with a luxuriant art, instead of leaving it to professionals, courts danger. In the second place, the complete absence of the popular ballad and an exclusive musical diet of aristocratic airs, as in *Troilus,* is an indication of the sickening softness and hotness that is the very fever of Troy. Dramatically, this extensive use of the air is an exceptional procedure with Shakespeare. For in *Troilus* the only other instance of song in the drama occurs in Act IV, where Pandarus performs fragments of another air.[11]

The absence of any ballads in the play is as unique as the absence of any leading role in the cast, as G. B. Shaw discerned so well in analyzing the reasons for the play's lack of success.[12] These exceptional features serve the same purpose, for this is a tragedy of the Trojan aristocracy, not of any individual, be he Troilus, Paris, or Hector, none of whose roles must

11 Shakespeare's words are here fitted to phrases of music from Thomas Morley's canzonet, "Hold out, my heart," reprinted in Bruce Pattison, *Poetry and Music of the English Renaissance,* London, 1948, p. 195.
12 G. B. Shaw, *Misalliance, The Dark Lady of the Sonnets,* New York, 1914, p. 139.

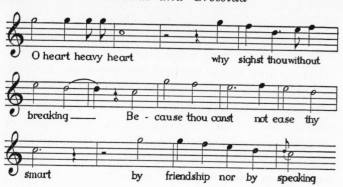

O heart heavy heart   why sighst thou without breaking ____ Be - cause thou canst not ease thy smart   by friendship nor by speaking

therefore obscure the over-all social satire. And the excess of cultivated hot music which begets hot love must destroy an entire class.

We may now realize how in *Troilus* two functions of music interpenetrate to heighten the drama. The broken consort and the air each fulfill two tasks: they influence man's disposition, and they characterize. However, the attribution of power and charm to these musical components of the drama must be qualified. It is true, they represent the kind of Italianate music that debases an Italianate English gentry. But that gentry is well disposed toward its own destruction before the first note of music sounds. The point is that the decadent knights have been *habitually* exposed to this voluptuous euphony and have thus lost their traditional customs, morals, and courage. On the other hand, we may say without qualification that the music expresses the tempers of the ruling class with uncanny accuracy. Thus, Shakespeare blends the magic and characterizing powers of music, the two main functions of the art of tones in his theater, and in the Elizabethan playhouse altogether. What makes his use of music so unique and so compelling is, not the introduction of novel resources, techniques, or even underlying philosophical concepts; rather, he accepts the storehouse which tradition and his contemporaries offer him and fashions from these materials a synthesis, an interplay of dramatic ingredients, past and present, which has remained, through the centuries, both his very own and unrivaled.

Macbeth as the
Imitation of an Action

※

By FRANCIS FERGUSSON

I PROPOSE to attempt to illustrate the view that *Macbeth* may be understood as "the imitation of an action," in approximately Aristotle's sense of this phrase. The word "action"—*praxis*—as Aristotle uses it in the *Poetics,* does not mean outward deeds or events, but something much more like "purpose" or "aim." Perhaps our word "motive" suggests most of its meaning. Dante (who in this respect is a sophisticated Aristotelian) uses the phrase *moto spiral,* spiritual movement, to indicate *praxis.* In Aristotle's own writings *praxis* is usually rational, a movement of the will in the light of the mind. But Dante's *moto spiral* refers to all modes of the spirit's life, all of its directions, or focuses, or motives, including those of childhood, dream, drunkenness, or passion, which are hardly rationalized at all. When using Aristotle's definition for the analysis of modern drama it is necessary to generalize his notion of action in this way, to include movements of the spirit in response to sensuous or emotionally charged images, as well as consciously willed purpose. But this seems to me a legitimate extension of the basic concept; and I do not think it does real violence to Aristotle's meaning.

Aristotle, in his *Psychology* and his *Ethics,* as well as in the *Poetics,* and Dante in the *Divine Comedy,* seem to imagine the psyche much as an amoeba looks under the microscope: moving toward what attracts it, continually changing direction or aim, and taking its shape and color from the object to which it is attached at the moment. This movement is "action"; and so we see that while the psyche is alive it always has action; and that this changing action in pursuit of real or imagined objects defines its mode of being moment by moment.

When Aristotle says that a tragedy is the imitation of an action, he is thinking of an action, or motive, which governs the psyche's life for a considerable length of time. Such an action is the quest for Laius's slayer in *Oedipus Rex,* which persists through the changing circumstances of the play. In this period of time, it has a beginning, a middle, and an end, which comes when the slayer is at last identified.

I remarked that action is not outward deeds or events; but on the other hand, there can be no action without resulting deeds. We guess at a man's action by way of what he does, his outward and visible deeds. We are aware that our own action, or motive, produces deeds of some sort as soon as it exists. Now the plot of a play is the arrangement of outward deeds or incidents, and the dramatist uses it, as Aristotle tells us, as the first means of imitating the action. He arranges a set of incidents which point to the action or

motive from which they spring. You may say that the
action is the spiritual content of the tragedy—the play-
wright's inspiration—and the plot defines its existence
as an intelligible *play*. Thus, you can never have a
play without both plot and action; yet the distinction
between plot and action is as fundamental as that between form and matter. The action is the matter; the
plot is the "first form," or, as Aristotle puts it, the
"soul" of the tragedy.

The dramatist imitates the action he has in mind,
first by means of the plot, then in the characters, and
finally in the media of language, music, and spectacle.
In a well-written play, if we understood it thoroughly,
we should perceive that plot, character, diction, and
the rest spring from the same source, or, in other words,
realize the same action or motive in the forms appropriate to their various media.

You will notice that this is a diagrammatic description of the perfect play, perfectly understood. Therefore one cannot hope to illustrate it perfectly, even
in the case of a play like *Macbeth. Macbeth,* however,
does impress most of its readers as having a powerful
and unmistakable unity of this kind: the plot, characters, and imagery all seem to spring from the one inspiration. It is that strong and immediately felt unity
which I rely on—and upon your familiarity with the
play. Not that I am so foolish as to suppose I grasp
the play completely or that I could persuade you of
my view of it in these few minutes. All I can attempt
is to suggest the single action which seems to me to be
the spiritual content of the play, and illustrate it, in

only a few of its metaphors, plot devices, and characterizations.

The action of the play as a whole is best expressed in a phrase which Macbeth himself uses in Act II, scene 3, the aftermath of the murder. Macbeth is trying to appear innocent, but everything he says betrays his clear sense of his own evil motivation, or action. Trying to excuse his murder of Duncan's grooms, he says,

The expedition of my violent love [for Duncan, he means]
Outran the pauser, reason.

It is the phrase "to outrun the pauser, reason," which seems to me to describe the action, or motive, of the play as a whole. Macbeth, of course, literally means that his love for Duncan was so strong and swift that it got ahead of his reason, which would have counseled a pause. But in the same way we have seen his greed and ambition outrun his reason when he committed the murder; and in the same way all of the characters, in the irrational darkness of Scotland's evil hour, are compelled in their action to strive beyond what they can see by reason alone. Even Malcolm and Macduff, as we shall see, are compelled to go beyond reason in the action which destroys Macbeth and ends the play.

But let me consider the phrase itself for a moment. To "outrun" reason suggests an impossible stunt, like lifting oneself by one's own bootstraps. It also suggests a competition or race, like those of nightmare, which cannot be won. As for the word "reason," Shakespeare associates it with nature and nature's order, in the individual soul, in society, and in the cosmos. To outrun reason is thus to violate nature itself, to lose the bearings of common sense and of custom, and to move into a spiritual realm bounded by the irrational darkness of hell one way, and the superrational grace of faith the other way. As the play develops before us, all the modes of this absurd, or evil, or supernatural action are attempted, the last being Malcolm's and Macduff's acts of faith.

In the first part of the play Shakespeare, as is his custom, gives us the intimate feel of this paradoxical striving beyond reason in a series of echoing tropes and images. I remind you of some of them, as follows.

From the first Witches' scene:

> When the battle's lost and won.
>
> Fair is foul and foul is fair.

From the "bleeding-sergeant" scene:

> Doubtful it stood;
> As two spent swimmers that do cling together
> And choke their art. . . .
> So from that spring whence comfort seem'd to come
> Discomfort swells.
>
> Confronted him with self-comparisons
> Point against point, rebellious arm 'gainst arm.
> What he hath lost noble Macbeth hath won.

From the second Witches' scene:

> So fair and foul a day.
>
> Lesser than Macbeth, and greater.
>
> His wonders and his praises do contend
> Which should be thine or his.

> This supernatural soliciting
> Cannot be ill, cannot be good.
>
> Nothing is, but what is not.

These are only a few of the figures which suggest the desperate and paradoxical struggle. They are, of course, not identical with each other or with outrunning reason, which seems to me the most general of all. But they all point to the "action" I mean, and I present them as examples of the imitation of action by means of the arts of language.

But notice that though these images themselves suggest the action, they also confirm the actions of the characters as these are shown in the story. The bleeding sergeant, for instance, is striving beyond reason and nature in his effort to report the battle—itself a bewildering mixture of victory and defeat—in spite of his wounds. Even the old King Duncan, mild though he is, is caught in the race and sees his relation to Macbeth competitively. "Thou art so far before," he tells Macbeth in the next scene, "That swiftest wing of recompense is slow To overtake thee." He then races Macbeth to his castle, whither the Messenger has outrun them both; and when he arrives, he is at once involved in a hollow competition with Lady Macbeth, to outdo her in ceremony.

I do not need to remind you of the great scenes preceding the murder, in which Macbeth and his Lady pull themselves together for their desperate effort. If you think over these scenes, you will notice that the Macbeths understand the action which begins here as a competition and a stunt, against reason and nature. Lady Macbeth fears her husband's human nature, as well as her own female nature, and therefore she fears the light of reason and the common daylight world. As for Macbeth, he knows from the first and he is engaged in an irrational stunt: "I have no spur To prick the sides of my intent, but only Vaulting ambition, which o'erleaps itself And falls on the other." In this sequence there is also the theme of outwitting or transcending time, an aspect of nature's order as we know it: catching-up the consequences, jumping the life to come, and the like. But this must suffice to remind you of the Macbeths' actions, which they paradoxically understand so well.

The Porter scene has been less thoroughly studied as a variation on the play's main action. But it is, in fact, a farcical and terrible version of "outrunning reason," a witty and very concentrated epitome of this absurd movement of spirit. The Porter first teases the knockers at the gate with a set of paradoxes, all of which present attempts to outrun reason; and he sees them all as ways into Hell. Henry N. Paul [1] has explained the contemporary references: the farmer who hanged himself on the expectation of plenty, the equivocator who swore both ways to commit treason for God's sake. When the Porter has admitted the knockers he ironically offers them lewd physical analogies for outrunning reason: drink as tempting lechery into a hopeless action; himself as wrestling with drink. The relation of the Porter to the knockers is like that of

[1] See *The Royal Play of Macbeth,* New York, 1950.

the Witches to Macbeth—he tempts them into Hell
with ambiguities. And the inebriation of drink and
lust, lewd and laughable as it is, is closely analogous
to the more terrible and spiritual intoxication of the
Macbeths.

Thus, in the first part of the play both the imagery
and the actions of the various characters indicate or
"imitate" the main action. Aristotle says the characters
are imitated "with a view to the action"—and the Porter, who has little importance in the story—is presented to reveal the action of the play as a whole in the
unexpected light of farcical analogies, contemporary
or lewd and physical.

Before I leave this part of the play I wish to point
out that the plot itself—"the arrangement or synthesis
of the incidents"—also imitates a desperate race. This
is partly a matter of the speed with which the main
facts are presented, partly the effect of simultaneous
movements like those of a race: Lady Macbeth is reading the letter at the same moment that her husband
and Duncan are rushing toward her. And the facts in
this part of the play are ambiguous in meaning and
even as facts.

These few illustrations must serve to indicate how
I understand the imitation of action in language,
character, and plot in the first two acts of the play.
Macbeth and his Lady are embarked on a race against
reason itself; and all Scotland, the "many" whose lives
depend upon the monarch, is precipitated into the
same darkness and desperate strife. Shakespeare's mon-
archs do usually color the spiritual life of their realms.

And we, who remember Hitlerite Germany, can understand that, I think. Even Hitler's exiles, like the refugees from Russian or Spanish tyranny, brought the shadow to this country with them.

I now wish to consider the action of the play at a later stage, in Act IV, scene 3. This is the moment which I mentioned before, the beginning of Malcolm's and Macduff's act of faith which will constitute the final variation on "outrunning reason." The scene is laid in England, whither Malcolm and Macduff have fled, and it immediately follows the murder of Macduff's wife and child. Like the exiles we have known in this country, Macduff and Malcolm, though in England, have brought Scotland's darkness with them. They have lost all faith in reason, human nature, and common sense, and can therefore trust neither themselves nor each other. They are met in the hope of forming an alliance, in order to get rid of Macbeth; and yet under his shadow everything they do seems unreasonable, paradoxical, improbable.

In the first part of the scene, you remember, Malcolm and Macduff fail to find any basis for mutual trust. Malcolm mistrusts Macduff because he has left his wife and child behind; Macduff quickly learns to mistrust Malcolm, because he first protests that he is unworthy of the crown, to test Macduff, and then suddenly reverses himself. The whole exchange is a tissue of falsity and paradox, and it ends in a sort of nightmarish paralysis.

At this point there is the brief interlude with the Doctor. The King's Evil and its cure and the graces which hang about the English throne are briefly described. Paul points out that this interlude may have been introduced to flatter James I; but however that may be, it is appropriate in the build of the scene as a whole. It marks the turning point, and it introduces the notion of the appeal by faith to Divine Grace which will reverse the evil course of the action when Malcolm and Macduff learn to outrun reason in that way, instead of by responding to the Witches' supernatural solicitations as Macbeth has done. Moreover, the Doctor in this scene, in whom religious and medical healing are associated, foreshadows the Doctor who will note Lady Macbeth's sleepwalking and describe it as a perturbation in nature which requires a cure beyond nature.

But to return to the scene. After the Doctor's interlude, Ross joins Malcolm and Macduff, bringing the latest news from Scotland. To greet him, Malcolm clearly states the action, or motive, of the scene as a whole: "Good God, betimes remove The means that make us strangers!" he says. Ross's chief news is, of course, Lady Macduff's murder. When he has gradually revealed that, and Macduff and Malcolm have taken it in, accepting some of the guilt, they find that the means that made them strangers has in fact been removed. They recognize themselves and each other once more, in a sober, but not nightmarish light. And at once they join in faith in their cause and prepare to hazard all upon the ordeal of battle, itself an appeal beyond reason. The scene, which in its opening sections moved very slowly, reflecting the demoralization of Malcolm and Macduff, ends hopefully, with brisk rhythms of speech which prepare the marching scenes to follow.

This tune goes manly. . . .

> Receive what hope you may:
> The night is long that never finds the day.

The whole scene is often omitted or drastically cut in production, and many critics have objected to it. They complain of its slowness, of the baroque overelaboration of Malcolm's protests, and of the fact that it is too long for what it tells us about the story. All we learn is that Malcolm and Macduff are joining the English army to attack Macbeth, and this information could have been conveyed much more quickly. In the first part of the play, and again after this scene, everything moves with the speed of a race; and one is tempted to say, at first, that in this scene Shakespeare lost the rhythm of his own play.

Now, one of the reasons I chose this scene to discuss is that it shows, as does the Porter scene, the necessity of distinguishing between plot and action. One cannot understand the function of the scene in the whole plot unless one remembers that the plot itself is there to imitate the action. It is then clear that this scene is the peripeteia, which is brought about by a series of recognitions. It starts with Malcolm and Macduff blind and impotent in Macbeth's shadow and ends when they have gradually learned to recognize themselves and each other even in that situation. "Outrunning reason" looks purely evil in the beginning, and at the end we see how it may be good, an act of faith beyond reason. The scene moves slowly at first because Shakespeare is imitating the action of groping in an atmosphere of the false and unnatural; yet we are aware all the while of continuing speed offstage, where

> each new morn
> New widows howl, new orphans cry, new sorrows
> Strike heaven on the face.

The scene is thus (within the rhythmic scheme of the whole play) like a slow eddy on the edge of a swift current. After this turning, or peripeteia, the actions of Malcolm and Macduff join the rush of the main race, to win. I admit that these effects might be hard to achieve in production, but I believe that good actors could do it.

Shakespeare's tragedies usually have a peripeteia in the fourth act, with scenes of suffering and prophetic or symbolic recognitions and epiphanies. In the fourth act of *Macbeth* the Witches' scene reveals the coming end of the action in symbolic shows; and this scene also, in another way, foretells the end. The last act, then, merely presents the literal facts, the wind-up of the plot, long felt as inevitable in principle. The fifth act of *Macbeth* shows the expected triumph of Malcolm's and Macduff's superrational faith. The wood does move; Macbeth does meet a man unborn of woman; and the paradoxical race against reason reaches its paradoxical end. The nightmare of Macbeth's evil version of the action is dissolved, and we are free to return to the familiar world, where reason, nature, and common sense still have their validity.

To sum up: my thesis is that *Macbeth* is the imitation of an action (or motive) which may be indicated by the phrase "to outrun the pauser, reason." I have tried to suggest how this action is presented in the metaphors, characters, and plot of the first two acts; and also in the peripeteia, with pathos and recognitions, the great scene between Malcolm, Macduff, and Ross.

I am painfully aware that these few illustrations are not enough to establish my thesis. Only a detailed analysis of the whole play might do that—and such an analysis would take hours of reading and discussion. But I think it would show that Aristotle was essentially right. He had never read *Macbeth,* and I suppose if he could he would find Shakespeare's Christian, or post-Christian, vision of evil hard to understand. But he saw that the art of drama is the art of imitating action; and this insight, confirmed and deepened by some of Aristotle's heirs, can still show us how to seek the unity of a play, even one which shows modes of the spirit's life undreamed of by Aristotle himself.

Literary Criticism:
Marvell's "Horatian Ode"

ψ

By CLEANTH BROOKS

THE EASIEST ERROR into which we may fall in defining the relationship between historical and critical
studies is illustrated by the preface of Maurice Kelley's
interesting book on Milton, *This Great Argument*.
For Kelley, the problem of exegesis is almost amusingly simple: we will read Milton's *Christian Doctrine*
to find out what Milton's ideas are, and then we shall
be able to understand his *Paradise Lost,* explaining the
tangled and difficult poetic document by means of the
explicit prose statement. But Kelley's argument rests
not only upon the assumption that the Milton who
wrote the *Christian Doctrine* was precisely and at all
points the same man who composed *Paradise Lost*—a
matter which, for all practical purposes, may well be
true; it rests upon the further and much more dan-
gerous assumption that Milton was able to *say* in *Paradise Lost* exactly what he intended to say; and that
what he supposed he had put into that poem is actually
to be found there. In short, Mr. Kelley tends to make
the assumption about poetry which most of us con-

stantly make; namely, that a poem is essentially a decorated and beautified piece of prose.

But I propose to deal here with a more modest example than Milton's epic. I propose to illustrate from Marvell's "Horatian Ode." If we follow the orthodox procedure, the obvious way to understand the "Ode" is to ascertain by historical evidence—by letters and documents of all kinds—what Marvell really thought of Cromwell, or, since Marvell apparently thought different things of Cromwell at different times, to ascertain the date of the "Ode," and then neatly fit it into the particular stage of Marvell's developing opinion of Cromwell. But this is at best a relatively coarse method which can hope to give no more than a rough approximation of the poem; and there lurk in it some positive perils. For to ascertain what Marvell the man thought of Cromwell, and even to ascertain what Marvell as poet consciously intended to say in his poem, will not prove that the poem actually says this, or all this, or merely this. This last remark, in my opinion, does not imply too metaphysical a notion of the structure of a poem. There is surely a sense in which any one must agree that a poem has a life of its own, and a sense in which it provides in itself the only criterion by which what it says can be judged. It is a commonplace that the poet sometimes writes better than he knows, and, alas, on occasion, writes worse than he knows. The history of English literature will furnish plenty of examples of both cases.

As a matter of fact, Marvell's "Ode" is not a shockingly special case. Indeed, I have chosen it for my

example, not because it is special—not because I hope
to reveal triumphantly that what it really says is something quite opposed to what we have supposed it to be
saying—but because it seems to me a good instance of
the normal state of affairs. Yet, even so, the "Ode" will
provide us with problems enough. To the scholar who
relies upon the conventional approach, the problems
become rather distressingly complicated.

Let us review the situation briefly. Hard upon his
composition of the "Ode" in 1650, Marvell had published in 1649 a poem "To his Noble Friend, Mr.
Richard Lovelace," and a poem "Upon the Death of
the Lord Hastings." Both Margoliouth and Legouis
find these poems rather pro-Royalist in sentiment and
certainly it is difficult to read them otherwise. If we add
to these poems the "Elegy upon the Death of My Lord
Francis Villiers," a Cavalier who was killed fighting
for the King in 1649, the Royalist bias becomes perfectly explicit. As Margoliouth puts it: "If [the elegy
on Villiers] is Marvell's, it is his one unequivocal royalist utterance; it throws into strong relief the transi-
tional character of *An Horatian Ode* where royalist
principles and admiration for Cromwell the Great
Man exist side by side. . . ."

A transition in views there must have been, but the
transition certainly cannot be graphed as a steadily rising curve when we take into account Marvell's next
poem, "Tom May's Death." May died in November,
1650. Thus we have the "Horatian Ode," which was almost certainly written in the summer of 1650, preceding by only a few months a poem in which Marvell

seems to slur at the Commander of the Parliamentary armies—either Essex or Fairfax—as "Spartacus," and to reprehend May himself as a renegade poet who has prostituted the mystery of the true poets. The curve of Marvell's political development shows still another surprising quirk when we recall that only a few months after his attack on May, Marvell was to be living under Spartacus Fairfax's roof, acting as tutor to his little daughter Mary.

Let me interrupt this summary to say that I am not forcing the evidence so as to crowd the historian into the narrowest and most uncomfortable corner possible. On the contrary, whatever forcing of the evidence has been done has been done by the editors and the historians. If we limit ourselves to historical evidence, it is possible to suppose that "Tom May's Death" was actually written on the Hill at Billborrow; and Margoliouth chooses early 1651 as the probable date for Marvell's arrival at Appleton House only because, as he says, " 'Tom May's Death' is not the sort of poem Marvell would have written under Fairfax's roof."

There is no need, in view of our purposes, to extend the review of Marvell's political development through the late 1650's with their Cromwellian poems or through the Restoration period with its vexed problems concerning which of the anti-court satires are truly, and which are falsely, ascribed to Marvell. The problem of Marvell's attitude through the years 1649–51 will provide sufficient scope for this examination of some of the relations and interrelations of the

historical approach and the critical approach. For
there is still another complication, which has received
less attention than it deserves. It is the curious fact that
the "Horatian Ode" in which Marvell seems to affirm
the ancient rights of the monarchy—

> Though Justice against Fate complain,
> And plead the antient Rights in vain—

is full of echoes of the poetry of Tom May, the poet
whom Marvell was, a few months later, to denounce
for having failed poetry in the hour of crisis:

> When the Sword glitters ore the Judges head,
> And fear the Coward Churchmen silenced,
> Then is the Poets time, 'tis then he drawes,
> And single fights forsaken Vertues cause.
> He, when the wheel of Empire, whirleth back,
> And though the World's disjointed Axel crack,
> Sings still of *antient Rights* and better Times,
> Seeks wretched good, arraigns successful Crimes.

The echoes of May's poetry, of course, may well have
been unconscious: to me it is significant that they are
from May's translation of Lucan's poem on the Roman
civil wars. (The relevant passage from Margoliouth's
notes will be found on pp. 129–30.) I must say that I
find the parallels quite convincing and that I am a little
surprised at Margoliouth's restraint in not pushing
his commentary further. For one is tempted to suppose
that in the year or so that followed the execution of
Charles, Marvell was obsessed with the problem of the
poet's function in such a crisis; that the poet May was
frequently in his mind through a double connection—
through the parallels between the English and the

Roman civil war, Lucan's poem on which May had translated, and through May's conduct as a partisan of the Commonwealth; and that the "Horatian Ode" and "Tom May's Death," though so different in tone, are closely related and come out of the same general state of mind. But to hazard all this is to guess at the circumstances of Marvell's composition of these poems. It can be only a guess, and, in any case, it takes us into a consideration of what must finally be a distinct problem: how the poem came to be; whereas our elected problem is rather: what the poem is. I am, by the way, in entire sympathy with the essay "The Intentional Fallacy," by W. K. Wimsatt and M. C. Beardsley, recently published in *The Sewanee Review*. We had best not try to telescope the separate problems of "the psychology of composition" and that of "objective evaluation." I have no intention of trying to collapse them here.

Well, what is "said" in the "Horatian Ode"? What is the speaker's attitude toward Cromwell and toward Charles? M. Legouis sees in the "Ode" a complete impartiality, an impartiality which is the product of Marvell's nonparticipation in the wars. Legouis can even speak of the poem as "ce monument d'indifférence en matière de régime politique." But the "Ode," though it may be a monument of impartiality, is not a monument of indifference. To read it in this fashion is to miss what seems to me to be a passionate interest in the issues, an interest which is manifested everywhere in the poem. It is true that we have no evidence that Marvell ever served in the civil war,

but we had better not leap to conclusions of his indifference from that. My own guess is that some young
Cavaliers who shed their blood for the King thought
and felt less deeply about the issues than does the
speaker of this poem. The tone is not that of a
"plague o' both your houses" nor is it that of "the
conflict provided glory enough to be shared by both
sides."

Mr. Margoliouth comes much closer to the point.
He sums up as follows: "The ode is the utterance of a
constitutional monarchist, whose sympathies have
been with the King, but who yet believes more in men
than in parties or principles, and whose hopes are fixed
now on Cromwell, seeing in him both the civic ideal
of a ruler without personal ambition, and the man of
destiny moved by and yet himself driving a power
which is above justice." This statement is plausible,
and for its purposes, perhaps just. But does it take us
very far—even on the level of understanding Marvell
the man? What sort of constitutional monarchist is it
who "believes more in men than in . . . principles"?
Or who can accept a "power which is above justice"? I
do not say that such a monarchist cannot exist. My
point is that Margoliouth's statement raises more problems than it solves. Furthermore, in what sense are the
speaker's hopes "fixed . . . on Cromwell"? And how
confident is he that Cromwell is "without personal
ambition"? I have quoted earlier Margoliouth's characterization of the "Ode" as a poem "where royalist
principles and admiration for Cromwell the Great
Man exist side by side." I think that they do exist side

by side, but if so, how are they related? Do they exist in separate layers, or are they somehow unified? Unified, in some sense, they must be if the "Ode" is a poem and not a heap of fragments.

I hope that my last statement indicates the kind of question which we finally have to face and answer. It is a problem of poetic organization. As such, it addresses itself properly to the critic. The historical scholars have not answered it, for it is a question which cannot be answered in terms of historical evidence. (This is not to say, of course, that the same man may not be both historical scholar and critic.) Moreover, I have already taken some pains to indicate how heavily the critic, on his part, may need to lean upon the historian. To put the matter into its simplest terms: the critic obviously must know what the words of the poem mean, something which immediately puts him in debt to the linguist; and since many of the words in this poem are proper nouns, in debt to the historian as well. I am not concerned to exalt the critic at the expense of specialists in other disciplines: on the contrary, I am only concerned to show that he has a significant function, and to indicate what the nature of that function is.

But I am not so presumptuous as to promise a solution to the problem. Instead, the reader will have to be content with suggestions—as to what the "Ode" is not saying, as to what the "Ode" may be saying—in short, with explorations of further problems. Many critical problems, of course, I shall have to pass over and some important ones I shall only touch upon. To illustrate:

there is the general Roman cast given to the "Ode."
Marvell has taken care to make no specifically Christian references in the poem. Charles is Caesar; Cromwell is a Hannibal; on the scaffold, Charles refuses to
call with "vulgar spight," not on God, but on "the
Gods," and so on. Or to point to another problem,
metaphors drawn from hunting pervade the poem.
Charles chases himself to Carisbrooke; Cromwell is
like the falcon; Cromwell will soon put his dogs in
"near/The *Caledonian* Deer." Or, to take up the
general organization of the poem: Marvell seems to
have used the celebrated stanzas on Charles's execution to divide the poem into two rather distinct parts:
first, Cromwell's rise to power; and second, Cromwell's
wielding of the supreme power. This scheme of division, by the way, I intend to make use of in the discussion that follows. But I shall try, in general, to limit
it to the specific problem of the speaker's attitude
toward Cromwell, subordinating other critical problems to this one, which is, I maintain, essentially a
critical problem too.

From historical evidence alone we would suppose
that the attitude toward Cromwell in this poem would
have to be a complex one. And this complexity is reflected in the ambiguity of the compliments paid to
him. The ambiguity reveals itself as early as the
second word of the poem. It is the "forward" youth
whose attention the speaker directs to the example
of Cromwell. "Forward" may mean no more than
"high-spirited," "ardent," "properly ambitious"; but
the *New English Dictionary* sanctions the possibility

that there lurks in the word the sense of "presumptuous," "pushing." The forward youth can no longer
now

> in the Shadows sing
> His Numbers languishing.

In the light of Cromwell's career, he must forsake the
shadows and his "Muses dear" and become the man
of action.

The speaker, one observes, does not identify Cromwell himself as the "forward youth," or say directly
that Cromwell's career has been motivated by a striving for fame. But the implications of the first two
stanzas do carry over to him. There is, for example, the
important word "so" to relate Cromwell to these
stanzas:

> So restless *Cromwel* could not cease. . . .

And "restless" is as ambiguous in its meanings as "forward," and in its darker connotations even more damn-
ing. For, though "restless" can mean "scorning indo-
lence," "willing to forego ease," it can also suggest the
man with a maggot in the brain. "To cease," used in-
transitively, is "to take rest, to be or remain at rest,"
and the *New English Dictionary* gives instances as late
as 1701. Cromwell's "courage high" will not allow him
to rest "in the inglorious Arts of Peace." And this
thirst for glory, merely hinted at here by negatives, is
developed further in the ninth stanza:

> Could by industrious Valour climbe
> To ruine the great Work of Time.

"Climb" certainly connotes a kind of aggressiveness.

In saying this we need not be afraid that we are reading into the word some smack of such modern phrases as "social climber." Marvell's translation of the second chorus of Seneca's *Thyestes* sufficiently attests that the word could have such associations for him:

> Climb at *Court* for me that will
> Tottering favors Pinacle;
> All I seek is to lye still.

Cromwell, on the other hand, does not seek to lie still—has sought something quite other than this. His valor is called—strange collocation—an "industrious valour," and his courage is too high to brook a rival:

> For 'tis all one to Courage high
> The Emulous or Enemy;
> And with such to inclose,
> Is more then to oppose.

The implied metaphor is that of some explosive which does more violence to that which encloses it, the powder to its magazine, for instance, than to some wall which merely opposes it—against which the charge is fired.

But the speaker has been careful to indicate that Cromwell's motivation has to be conceived of as more complex than any mere thirst for glory. He has even pointed this up. The forward youth is referred to as one who "would appear"—that is, as one who wills to leave the shadows of obscurity. But restless Cromwell "could not cease"—for Cromwell it is not a question of will at all, but of a deeper compulsion. Restless Cromwell could not cease, if he would.

Indeed, the lines that follow extend the suggestion

that Cromwell is like an elemental force—with as
little will as the lightning bolt, and with as little conscience:

> And, like the three-fork'd Lightning, first
> Breaking the Clouds where it was nurst,
>   Did thorough his own Side
>   His fiery way divide.

We are told that the last two lines refer to Cromwell's struggle after Marston Moor with the leaders
of the Parliamentary party. Doubtless they do, and the
point is important for our knowledge of the poem. But
what is more important is that we be fully alive to the
force of the metaphor. The clouds have bred the lightning bolt, but the bolt tears its way through the clouds,
and goes on to blast the head of Caesar himself. As
Margoliouth puts it: "The lightning is conceived as
tearing through the side of his own body the cloud." In
terms of the metaphor, then, Cromwell has not spared
his own body: there is no reason therefore to be surprised that he has not spared the body of Charles.

I do not believe that I overemphasized the speaker's
implication that Cromwell is a natural force. A few
lines later the point is reinforced with another naturalistic figure, an analogy taken from physics:

> Nature that hateth emptiness,
> Allows of penetration less:
>   And therefore must make room
>   Where greater Spirits come . . .

The question of right, the imagery insists, is beside
the point. If nature will not tolerate a power vacuum,
no more will it allow two bodies to occupy the same

space. (It is amusing, by the way, that Marvell has boldly introduced into his analogy borrowed from physics the nonphysical term "Spirits"; yet I do not think that the clash destroys the figure. Since twenty thousand angels can dance on the point of a needle, two spirits, even though one of them is a greater spirit, ought to be able to occupy the same room. But two spirits, as Marvell conceives of spirits here, will jostle one another, and one must give way. True, the greater spirit is immaterial, but he is no pale abstraction—he is all air and fire, the "force of angry Heavens flame." The metaphor ought to give less trouble to the reader of our day than it conceivably gave to readers bred up on Newtonian physics.)

What are the implications for Charles? Does the poet mean to imply that Charles has angered heaven—that he has merited his destruction? There is no suggestion that Cromwell is a thunderbolt hurled by an angry Jehovah—or even by an angry Jove. The general emphasis on Cromwell as an elemental force is thoroughly relevant here to counter this possible misreading. Certainly, in the lines that follow there is nothing to suggest that Charles has angered heaven, or that the Justice which complains against his fate is anything less than justice.

I began this examination of the imagery with the question, "What is the speaker's attitude toward Cromwell?" We have seen that the speaker more than once hints at his thirst for glory:

> So restless *Cromwel* could not cease . . .
> Could by industrious Valour climbe . . .

But we have also seen that the imagery tends to view Cromwell as a natural phenomenon, the bolt bred in the cloud. Is there a contradiction? I think not. Cromwell's is no vulgar ambition. If his valor is an "industrious Valour," it contains plain valor too of a kind perfectly capable of being recognized by any Cavalier:

> What Field of all the Civil Wars,
> Where his were not the deepest Scars?

If the driving force has been a desire for glory, it is a glory of that kind which allows a man to become dedicated and, in a sense, even selfless in his pursuit of it. Moreover, the desire for such glory can become so much a compulsive force that the man does not appear to act by an exercise of his personal will but seems to become the very will of something else. There is in the poem, it seems to me, at least one specific suggestion of this sort:

> But through adventrous War
> Urged his active Star. . . .

Cromwell is the marked man, the man of destiny, but he is not merely the man governed by his star. Active though it be, he cannot remain passive, even in relation to it: he is not merely urged by it, but himself urges it on.

Yet, if thus far Cromwell has been treated as naked force, something almost too awesome to be considered as a man, the poet does not forget that after all he is a man too—that "the force of angry Heavens flame" is embodied in a human being:

> And, if we would speak true,
> Much to the Man is due.

The stanzas that follow proceed to define and praise that manliness—the strength, the industrious valor, the cunning. (You will notice that I reject the interpretation which would paraphrase "Much to the Man is due" as "After all, Cromwell has accomplished much that is good." Such an interpretation could sort well enough with Legouis's picture of Marvell as the cold and detached honest broker between the factions: unfortunately it will not survive a close scrutiny of the grammar and the general context in which the passage is placed.)

One notices that among the virtues composing Cromwell's manliness, the speaker mentions his possession of the "wiser art":

> Where, twining subtile fears with hope,
> He wove a Net of such a scope,
>   That *Charles* himselfe might chase
>   To *Caresbrooks* narrow case.

On this point Cromwell has been cleared by all the modern historians (except perhaps Mr. Hilaire Belloc). Charles's flight to Carisbrooke Castle, as it turned out, aided Cromwell, but Cromwell could have hardly known that it would; and there is no evidence that he cunningly induced the King to flee to Carisbrooke. Royalist pamphleteers, of course, believed that Cromwell did, and used the item in their general bill of damnation against Cromwell. How does the speaker use it here—to damn or to praise? We tend to answer, "To praise." But then it behooves us to notice what is being praised. The things praised are Cromwell's talents as such—the tremendous disciplined powers which Cromwell brought to bear against the King.

For the end served by those powers, the speaker has no praise at all. Rather he has gone out of his way to insist that Cromwell was deaf to the complaint of Justice and its pleading of the "antient Rights." The power achieved by Cromwell is a "forced Pow'r"— a usurped power. On this point the speaker is unequivocal. I must question therefore Margoliouth's statement that Marvell sees in Cromwell "the man of destiny moved by . . . a power that is above justice." Above justice, yes, in the sense that power is power and justice is not power. The one does not insure the presence of the other. Charles has no way to vindicate his "helpless Right," but it is no less Right because it is helpless. But the speaker, though he is not a cynic, is a realist. A kingdom cannot be held by mere pleading of the "antient Rights":

> But those do hold or break
> As Men are strong or weak.

In short, the more closely we look at the "Ode," the more clearly apparent it becomes that the speaker has chosen to emphasize Cromwell's virtues as a man, and likewise, those of Charles as a man. The poem does not debate which of the two was right, for that issue is not even in question. In his treatment of Charles, then, the speaker no more than Charles himself attempts to vindicate his "helpless Right." Instead, he emphasizes his dignity, his fortitude, and what has finally to be called his consummate good taste. The portraits of the two men beautifully supplement each other. Cromwell is—to use Aristotle's distinction—the man of character, the man of action, who "does both act and know." Charles, on the other hand, is the man of passion, the man who is acted upon, the man who knows how to suffer. The contrast is pointed up in half a dozen different ways.

Cromwell, acted upon by his star, is not passive but actually urges his star. Charles in "acting"—in chasing away to Carisbrooke—actually is passive—performs the part assigned to him by Cromwell. True, we can read "chase" as an intransitive verb (the *New English Dictionary* sanctions this use for the period): "that Charles himself might hurry to Carisbrooke." But the primary meaning asserts itself in the context: "that Charles might chase himself to Carisbrooke's narrow case." For this hunter, now preparing to lay his dogs in "near/The *Caledonian* Deer," the royal quarry has dutifully chased itself.

Even in the celebrated stanzas on the execution, there is ironic realism as well as admiration. In this fullest presentation of Charles as king, he is the player king, the king acting in a play. He is the "Royal Actor" who knows his assigned part and performs it with dignity. He truly adorned the "Tragick Scaffold"

> While round the armed Bands
> Did clap their bloody hands.

The generally received account is that the soldiers clapped their hands so as to make it impossible for Charles's speech to be heard. But in the context this reference to hand-clapping supports the stage meta-

phor. What is being applauded? Cromwell's resolution
in bringing the King to a deserved death? Or Charles's
resolution on the scaffold as he suffered that death?
Marvell was too good a poet to resolve the ambiguity.
It is enough that he makes the armed bands applaud.

It has not been pointed out, I believe, that Robert
Wild, in his poem on "The Death of Mr. Christopher
Love," has echoed a pair of Marvell's finest lines. Love
was beheaded by Cromwell on August 22, 1651. In
Wild's poem, Marvell's lines

> But with his keener Eye
> The Axes edge did try

become: "His keener words did their sharp Ax ex-
ceed." The point is of no especial importance except
that it indicates, since Wild's poem was evidently written shortly after Love's execution, that in 1651 the
"Horatian Ode" was being handed about among the
Royalists. For Wild was that strange combination, an
English Presbyterian Royalist.

I have pointed out earlier that the second half of the
poem begins here with the reference to

> that memorable Hour
> Which first assur'd the forced Pow'r.

Cromwell is now the *de facto* head of the state, and the
speaker, as a realist, recognizes that fact. Cromwell is
seen henceforth, not primarily in his character as the
destroyer of the monarchy, but as the agent of the new
state that has been erected upon the dead body of the
King. The thunderbolt simile, of the first part of the
poem, gives way here to the falcon simile in this second

part of the poem. The latter figure revises and quali-
fies the former: it repeats the suggestion of ruthless
energy and power, but Cromwell falls from the sky
now, not as the thunderbolt, but as the hunting hawk.
The trained falcon is not a wanton destroyer, nor an irresponsible one. It knows its master: it is perfectly disciplined:

> She, having kill'd, no more does search,
> But on the next green Bow to pearch . . .

The speaker's admiration for Cromwell the man
culminates, it seems to me, here. Cromwell might
make the Fame his own; he *need* not present kingdoms
to the state. He might assume the crown rather than
crowning each year. Yet he forbears:

> Nor yet grown stiffer with Command,
> But still in the *Republick's* hand . . .

Does the emphasis on "still" mean that the speaker is
surprised that Cromwell has continued to pay homage
to the republic? Does he imply that Cromwell may not
always do so? Perhaps not: the emphasis is upon the
fact that he need not obey and yet does. Yet the compliment derives its full force from the fact that the
homage is not forced, but voluntary and even somewhat unexpected. And a recognition of this point implies the recognition of the possibility that Cromwell
will not always so defer to the commonwealth.

And now what of the republic which Cromwell so
ruthlessly and efficiently serves? What is the speaker's
attitude toward it? To begin with, the speaker recognizes that its foundations rest upon the bleeding head

of Charles. The speaker is aware, it is true, of the Roman analogy, and the English state is allowed the benefit of that analogy. But it is well to notice that the speaker does not commit himself to the opinion that the bleeding head is a happy augury:

> And yet in that the *State*
> Foresaw it's happy Fate.

The Roman state was able to take it as a favorable omen, and was justified by the event. With regard to the speaker himself, it seems to me more to the point to notice what prophecy he is willing to commit himself to. He does not prophesy peace. He is willing to predict that England, under Cromwell's leadership, will be powerful in war, and will strike fear into the surrounding states:

> What may not then our *Isle* presume
> While Victory his Crest does plume!
> 　What may not others fear
> 　If thus he crown each year!

Specifically, he predicts a smashing victory over the Scots.

But what of the compliments to Cromwell on his ruthlessly effective campaign against the Irish? Does not the speaker succumb, for once, to a bitter and biased patriotism, and does this not constitute a blemish upon the poem?

> And now the *Irish* are asham'd
> To see themselves in one Year tam'd:
> 　So much one Man can do,
> 　That does both act and know.

> They can affirm his Praises best,
> And have, though overcome, confest
> How good he is, how just. . . .

Margoliouth glosses the word "confessed" as follows: "Irish testimony in favor of Cromwell at this moment is highly improbable. Possibly there is a reference to the voluntary submission of part of Munster with its English colony." But surely Margoliouth indulges in understatement. The most intense partisan of Cromwell would have had some difficulty in taking the lines without some inflection of grim irony. The final appeal in this matter, however, is not to what Marvell the Englishman must have thought, or even to what Marvell the author must have intended, but rather to the full context of the poem itself. In that context, the lines in question can be read ironically, and the earlier stanzas sanction that reading. Cromwell's energy, activity, bravery, resolution—even what may be called his efficiency—are the qualities that have come in for praise, not his gentleness or his mercy. The Irish, indeed, are best able to affirm such praise as has been accorded to Cromwell; and they know from experience "how good he is, how just," for they have been blasted by the force of angry Heaven's flame, even as Charles has been. But I do not mean to turn the passage into sarcasm. The third quality which the speaker couples with goodness and justice is fitness "for highest Trust," and the goodness and justice of Cromwell culminate in this fitness. But the recommendation to trust has reference not to the Irish, but to the English state. The Irish are quite proper authorities on Cromwell's trustworthiness in this regard, for they have come to know him as the completely dedicated instrument of that state whose devotion to the purpose in hand is unrelenting and unswerving.

To say all this is not to suggest that Marvell shed any unnecessary tears over the plight of the Irish, or even to imply that he was not happy, as one assumes most Englishmen were, to have the Irish rebellion crushed promptly and efficiently. It is to say that the passage fits into the poem—a poem which reveals itself to be no panegyric on Cromwell but an unflinching analysis of the Cromwellian character.

The wild Irish have been tamed, and now the Pict will no longer be able to shelter under his particolored mind. It is the hour of decision, and the particolored mind affords no protection against the man who "does both act and know." In Cromwell's mind there are no conflicts, no teasing mixture of judgments. Cromwell's is not only an "industrious valour," but a "sad valour." Margoliouth glosses "sad" as "steadfast," and no doubt he is right. But sad can mean "sober" also, and I suspect that in this context, with its implied references to Scottish plaids, it means also drab of hue. It is also possible that the poet here glances at one of Virgil's transferred epithets, *maestum timorem,* sad fear, the fear that made the Trojans sad. Cromwell's valor is *sad* in that the Scots will have occasion to rue it.

Thus far the speaker has been content to view Cromwell from a distance, as it were, against the background of recent history. He has referred to him consistently in the third person. But in the last two stanzas, he addresses Cromwell directly. He salutes him as "the Wars and Fortunes Son." It is a great compliment: Cromwell is the son of the wars in that he is the master of battle, and he seems fortune's own son in the success that has constantly waited upon him. But we do not wrench the lines if we take them to say also that Cromwell is the creature of the wars and the product of fortune. The imagery of the early stanzas which treats Cromwell as a natural phenomenon certainly lends support to this reading. Cromwell can claim no sanction for his power in "antient Rights." His power has come out of the wars and the troubled times. I call attention to the fact that we do not have to choose between readings: the readings do not mutually exclude each other: they support each other, and this double interpretation has the whole poem behind it.

Cromwell is urged to march "indefatigably on." The advice is good advice; but it is good advice because any other course of action is positively unthinkable. Indeed, to call it advice at all is perhaps to distort it: though addressed to Cromwell, it partakes of quiet commentary as much as of exhortation. After all, it is restless Cromwell who is being addressed. If he could not cease "in the inglorious Arts of Peace" when his "highest plot" was "to plant the Bergamot," one cannot conceive of his ceasing now in the hour of danger.

> And for the last effect
> Still keep thy Sword erect.

Once more the advice (or commentary) is seriously intended, but it carries with it as much of warning as it does of approval. Those who take up the sword shall perish by the sword: those who have achieved their power on contravention of ancient rights by the sword can only expect to maintain their power by the sword.

What kind of sword is it that is able to "fright the spirits of the shady night"? Margoliouth writes: "The cross hilt of the sword would avert the spirits. . . ." But the speaker makes it quite plain that it is not merely the spirits of the shady night that Cromwell will have to fight as he marches indefatigably on. It will not be enough to hold the sword aloft as a ritual sword, an emblematic sword. The naked steel will still have to be used against bodies less diaphanous than spirits. If there is any doubt as to this last point, Marvell's concluding lines put it as powerfully and explicitly as it can be put:

> The same *Arts* that did *gain*
> A *Pow'r* must it *maintain*.

But, I can imagine someone asking, What is the final attitude toward Cromwell? Is it ultimately one of approval or disapproval? Does admiration overbalance condemnation? Or, is the "Ode," after all, merely a varied Scottish plaid, the reflection of Marvell's own particolored mind—a mind which had not been finally "made up" with regard to Cromwell? I think that enough has been said to make it plain that there is no easy, pat answer to such questions. There is a unified total attitude, it seems to me; but it is so complex that we may oversimplify and distort its complexity by the way in which we put the question. The request for some kind of summing up is a natural one, and I have no wish to try to evade it. For a really full answer, of course, one must refer the questioner to the poem itself; but one can at least try to suggest some aspects of the total attitude.

I would begin by reemphasizing the dramatic character of the poem. It is not a statement—an essay on "Why I cannot support Cromwell" or on "Why I am now ready to support Cromwell." It is a poem essentially dramatic in its presentation, which means that it is diagnostic rather than remedial, and eventuates, not in a course of action, but in contemplation. Perhaps the best way therefore in which to approach it is to conceive of it as, say, one conceives of a Shakespearean tragedy. Cromwell is the usurper who demands and commands admiration. What, for example, is our attitude toward Macbeth? We assume his guilt, but there are qualities which emerge from his guilt which properly excite admiration. I do not mean that the qualities palliate his guilt or that they compensate for his guilt. They actually come into being through his guilt, but they force us to exalt him even as we condemn him. I have chosen an extreme example. I certainly do not mean to imply that in writing the "Ode" Marvell had Shakespeare's tragedy in mind. What I am trying to point to is this: that the kind of honesty and insight and whole-mindedness which we associate with tragedy is to be found to some degree in all great poetry and is to be found in this poem.

R. P. Warren once remarked to me that Marvell has constantly behind him in his poetry the achievement of Elizabethan drama with its treatment of the human will as seen in the perspective of history. He had in mind some of the lyrics, but the remark certainly applies fully to the "Ode." The poet is thoroughly conscious of the drama, and consciously makes use of dramatic perspective. Charles, as we have seen, becomes the "Royal Actor," playing his part on the "Tragick Scaffold." But the tragedy of Charles is merely glanced at. The poem is Cromwell's—Cromwell's tragedy, the first three acts of it, as it were, which is not a tragedy of failure but of success.

Cromwell is the truly kingly man who is *not* king—whose very virtues conduce to kingly power and almost force kingly power upon him. It is not any fumbling on the poet's part which causes him to call Cromwell "a Caesar" before the poem ends, even though he has earlier appropriated that name to Charles. *Both* men are Caesar, Charles the wearer of the purple, and Cromwell, the invincible general, the inveterate campaigner, the man "that does both act and know." Cromwell is the Caesar who must refuse the crown—whose glory it is that he is willing to refuse the crown—but who cannot enjoy the reward and the security that a crown affords. The tension between the speaker's admiration for the kingliness which has won Cromwell the power and his awareness that the power can be maintained only by a continual exertion of these talents for kingship—this tension is never relaxed. Cromwell is not of royal blood—he boasts a higher and a baser pedigree: he is the "Wars and Fortunes Son." He cannot rest because he is restless Cromwell. He must march indefatigably on, for he cannot afford to become fatigued. These implications enrich and qualify an insight into Cromwell which is as heavily freighted with admiration as it is with a great condemnation. But the admiration and the condemnation do not cancel each other. They define each other; and because there is responsible definition, they reinforce each other.

Was this, then, the attitude of Andrew Marvell, born 1621, sometime student at Cambridge, returned traveler and prospective tutor, toward Oliver Cromwell in the summer of 1650? The honest answer must be: I do not know. I have tried to read the poem, the "Horatian Ode," not Andrew Marvell's mind. That seems sensible to me in view of the fact that we have the poem, whereas the attitude held by Marvell at any particular time must be a matter of inference—even though I grant that the poem may be put in as part of the evidence from which we draw inferences. True, we do know that Marvell was capable of composing the "Ode" and I must concede that that fact may tell us a great deal about Marvell's attitude toward Cromwell. I think it probably does. I am not sure, for reasons given earlier in this paper, that it tells us everything: there is the problem of the role of the unconscious in the process of composition, there is the possibility of the poet's having written better than he knew, there is even the matter of the happy accident. I do not mean to overemphasize these matters. I do think, however, that it is wise to maintain the distinction between what total attitude is manifested in the poem and the attitude of the author as citizen.

Yet, though I wish to maintain this distinction, I do not mean to hide behind it. The total attitude realized in the "Ode" does not seem to me monstrously inhuman in its complexity. It could be held by human beings, in my opinion. Something very like it apparently was. Listen, for example, to the Earl of Clarendon's judgment on Cromwell:

He was one of those men, quos vitupare ne inimici quidem possunt, nisi ut simul laudent [whom not even their enemies can inveigh against without at the same time praising them], for he could never have done halfe that mischieve, without great partes of courage and industry and judgement, and he must have had a wonderful understandinge in the nature and humours of men, and as greate a dexterity in the applyinge them, who from a private and obscure birth (though of a good family), without interest of estate, allyance or frenshippes, could rayse himselfe to such a height, and compounde and kneade such opposite and contradictory humours and interests, into a consistence, that contributed to his designes and to ther owne distruction, whilst himselfe grew insensibly powerfull enough, to cutt off those by whom he had climed, in the instant, that they projected to demolish ther owne buildinge. . . .

He was not a man of bloode, and totally declined Machiavells methode . . . it was more then once proposed, that ther might be a generall massacre of all the royall party, as the only expedient to secure the government, but Crumwell would never consent to it, it may be out of to much contempt of his enimyes; In a worde, as he had all the wikednesses against which damnation is denounced and for which Hell fyre is praepared, so he had some virtues, which have caused the memory of some men in all ages to be celebrated, and he will be looked upon by posterity, as a brave, badd man.

The resemblance between Clarendon's judgment and that reflected in the "Ode" is at some points so remarkable that one wonders whether Clarendon had not seen and been impressed by some now lost manuscript of the "Ode": "Who from a private and obscure birth"—"Who, from his private Gardens, where/He liv'd reserved and austere"—"could rayse himself to such a height . . . by whome he had climed"—"Could by industrious Valour climbe," and so on and so forth. But I do not want to press the suggestion of influence of Marvell on Clarendon. Indeed, it makes for my general point to discount the possibility. For what I am anxious to emphasize is that the attitude of the "Ode" is not inhuman in its Olympian detachment, that something like it could be held by a human being, and by a human being of pronounced Royalist sympathies.

I have argued that the critic needs the help of the historian—all the help that he can get—but I have insisted that the poem has to be read as a poem—that what it "says" is a question for the critic to answer, and that no amount of historical evidence as such can finally determine what the poem says. But if we do read the poem successfully, the critic may on occasion be able to make a return on his debt to the historian. If we have read the "Ode" successfully—*if*, I say, for I am far from confident—it may be easier for us to understand how the man capable of writing the

"Ode" was also able to write "Tom May's Death" and "On Appleton House" and indeed, years later, after the Restoration, the statement: "Men ought to have trusted God; they ought and might have trusted the King."

Since completing this essay, I have come upon a further (see p. 116) item which would suggest that the "Horatian Ode" was circulating among Royalists—not Puritans—in the early 1650's. The stanza form of the "Horatian Ode" was used only once by Marvell (in this poem) and does not seem to occur in English poetry prior to Marvell. Margoliouth and Legouis think it probable that this stanza was Marvell's own invention. Perhaps it was. But in Sir Richard Fanshawe's translation of Horace's Odes (*Selected Parts of Horace . . . Now newly put into English,* London, 1652) the "Horatian Ode" stanza is used several times. If Marvell invented the stanza in the summer of 1650, he must have been in close association with Fanshawe for Fanshawe to have borrowed and made use of the stanza so frequently in poems which were to be in print two years later. I suspect that Marvell borrowed the stanza from Fanshawe. Fanshawe had begun to publish translations of Horace (though none in this stanza pattern) as early as 1648 in the volume which contained his translation of *Il Pastor Fido.* But in either case a Royalist connection for Marvell is implied, for Fanshawe (1608–66) was a fervent and active Royalist throughout the war, and after the Restoration was a trusted servant of Charles II.

The following notes appear in H. M. Margoliouth's edition of *The Poems and Letters of Andrew Marvell* (Oxford: Clarendon Press, 1927), I, 237–38:

A correspondent in *The Times Literary Supplement* (29 January 1920) compares with ll. 9–16 of this Ode Lucan, *Pharsalia,* i. 144 *et seq.* . . .

Marvell perhaps had in mind both the Latin (cf. successus urgere suos and "Urg'd his active Star") and Tom May's translation, which here reads as follows (2nd edition, 1631):

But restlesse valour, and in warre a shame
Not to be Conquerour; fierce, not curb'd at all,
Ready to fight, where hope, or anger call,
His forward Sword; confident of successe,
And bold the favour of the gods to presse:
Orethrowing all that his ambition stay,
And loves that ruine should enforce his way;
As lightning by the wind forc'd from a cloude
Breakes through the wounded aire with thunder loud,
Disturbes the Day, the people terrifyes,
And by a light oblique dazels our eyes,
Not *Joves* owne Temple spares it; when no force,
No barre can hinder his prevailing course,
Great waste, as foorth it sallyes and retires,
It makes and gathers his dispersed fires.

Note the verbal resemblances, "restlesse valour" and "industrious Valour," "forward Sword" and "The forward Youth," "lightning . . . from a cloude Breakes" and "Lightning . . . Breaking the Clouds." Further I suggest with diffidence that the striking phrase "active Star" owes something to the chance neighbourhood of the two words in another passage in the same book of May's translation (*Pharsalia,* i. 229–32):

. . . the active Generall
Swifter than Parthian back-shot shaft, or stone
From Balearick Slinger, marches on

T' invade Ariminum; when every star
Fled from th' approaching Sunne but Lucifer . . .

Caesar is up betimes, marching when only the morning star is in the sky: Cromwell urges *his* "active star."

Sir Edward Ridley, carrying on the correspondence in *The Times Literary Supplement* (5 February 1920), points out further a likeness between Marvell's account of the death of Charles I and *Pharsalia,* viii. 613–17 (the death of Pompey):

ut vidit comminus ensem
involvit vultus atque indignatus apertum
fortunae praestare caput, tunc lumina pressit
continuitque animam, ne quas effundere voces
posset et aeternam fletu corrumpere famam . . .

John Milton

By DOUGLAS BUSH

IN TRYING to assess the value of biographical evidence
for the understanding of Milton's poetry, we may
start with two or three obvious general facts.[1] Thanks
to Milton's own writings, the early biographers, and
the labors of Masson and modern scholars, we know
more about him than we know about any other Englishman of his century, or indeed about any Englishman before him. Moreover, to put much the same fact
in a different way, Milton was not an innocent by-
stander but an active revolutionary, and his poetry is
far outweighed in bulk by his prose writings. The
most direct and valuable insights into his life, character, and work are, of course, given by the autobio-
graphical material in both prose and verse; and the
whole body of his prose, as the fullest record of his intellectual and spiritual development, is very important in itself and forms the best introduction to
and commentary upon his major poems. But I am as-

[1] This paper was originally written for delivery only and has been
abridged and somewhat revised for publication.

suming that the framers of this program were concerned with Milton's poetry and took his prose writings for granted.

Milton's public career and prose works have contributed a good deal to prejudice against the man and the thinker and, consequently, against the poet. He has in fact been a signal, perhaps a unique, victim of the physical law enunciated by his great contemporary —that pressure exerted anywhere upon a mass of fluid is transmitted undiminished in all directions, and so forth. For instance, the author of "Methought I saw my late espoused Saint" has been charged with "a Turkish contempt of females," although he only shared the general and traditional view of woman's inferiority to man in the chain of being, and although he held an uncommonly high view of man, woman, and marriage. He has suffered from the traditional belief that he wrote his first tract on divorce during his honeymoon; but modern investigation, especially by Mr. B. A. Wright, of the merely circumstantial accounts of his marriage, has yielded virtual proof that it occurred in 1642 and not a year later, so that one unlovely blot has been wiped out. Then, Milton being by definition a great egoist and rebel, it has been said again and again that his pamphlets were not disinterested but were the products of personal grievances. Obviously Milton's personal feelings were involved, as personal feelings are involved in any earnest attempt to sway the public mind; but modern scholarship has considerably modified this evidence of "egoism" by showing that Milton was dealing with subjects to which he had earlier given disinterested thought.

These are only a few random—and mild—examples of the bits of mud which have been thrown so freely at Milton and which, coalescing, have provided the common and forbidding image of a great man with feet of clay. Whatever Milton's actual faults of character, it is a curious thing that his high and rare measure of virtue and righteousness causes much more offense than the scarlet sins of other writers. Literary critics can condemn the man without any evidence at all, and some scholars have been moved to magnify or manufacture evidence. Since the worst charges have been amply refuted, and indeed refute themselves, we need not go into them. I bring up the matter partly because, as I said, prejudice against Milton's personal character has colored so much criticism, and partly because it raises the large general question of how far the integrity of the man is bound up with the integrity of the artist. There are many critics and scholars who would apparently deny any relation between the two (except of course in regard to Milton). I myself hold the perhaps naïve belief that the integrity of the artist is not independent of the integrity of the man, though in saying that I do not mean to say what would be still more naïve, that integrity means moral blamelessness. But it seems to me no less naïve to assume, as a good many critics seem to do, that a shabby or dissolute life and character are a kind of guarantee of artistic integrity and that virtue is a fatal impediment. In the present instance, if we were forced to believe that Milton was a knave, or even a self-righteous hypocrite, I do not see how the religious and moral edifice of his poetry could stand unshaken. There are no doubt many poets, from Villon to Baudelaire and Hart Crane, who may in hell conceive a heavenly vision, but Milton is not of that kind; he is all of a piece.

To turn to the poetry, we may observe how biographical evidence has been used by a few critics and scholars. The first name that comes to mind is Dr. Johnson. Everyone knows both how greatly, at times, Johnson could write of Milton, and also how far his view of the man and the pamphleteer was colored by Anglican and Tory prejudice. He saw Milton as a proud egoist, a misguided and violent rebel against the church, a surly and acrimonious republican. But Johnson, whether right or wrong, was always an honest critic as well as an honest man. The notorious errors and defects in his account of Milton's poetry are not caused by the carrying over of personal, religious, and political prejudice into criticism; they come rather from want of sensibility and perception, a want aggravated by some articles of his literary creed.

If we jump down to the nineteen twenties and nineteen thirties, we find a hue and cry against Milton, led by such poets as Mr. Pound and Mr. Eliot and supported by their critical followers and a few others.[2] I recently gave some discussion to this subject in a small

2 In incidental comments Mr. Eliot has been moving away from his earlier position and in his recent lecture on Milton he makes a considerable retraction.

book on *Paradise Lost* and cannot repeat it here. But we may remind ourselves briefly that this criticism was not at all disinterested; it started with the object of dethroning Milton in favor of "metaphysical" poets, from Dante and Donne to Pound and Eliot. Although modern criticism professes a lofty concern with an author's works and not his personal character, in the criticism of Milton no holds were barred. A prejudice against the man was used as a ready and easy way to establish a prejudice against his poetry. Milton was presented as a powerful but repellent personality who expounded repellent beliefs and ideas in verse of repellent organization and texture. Most of the dicta—one cannot call them arguments—directed against the man and the thinker were taken over uncritically from the nineteenth century; the only novelty was a dislike of the Miltonic style which the nineteenth century had glorified as sublime. Outside of this small but very assertive movement there were, of course, disinterested critics concerned only with understanding Milton's art, but it was the critics in the movement who had the ear of the highbrow reader.

If literary scholars have not approached such extremes of hostile prejudice, they have not always been proof against their own idols of the cave. For instance, M. Saurat's Milton, as I think Mr. Tillyard has remarked somewhere, comes to seem very much like a nineteenth-century French anticlerical. We may look somewhat closely at Saurat's work because he was a conspicuous exemplar of the use of biographical evidence and because he took a provocative and important part in the revaluation of Milton. The early twentieth century inherited the romantic and nineteenth-century habit of ignoring or disparaging Milton's beliefs and ideas in order to "save" the poetry. When the anti-Miltonist critics were summarily denouncing Milton's beliefs and ideas in good set nineteenth-century terms, they were, as I said, rather out of date. Such scholars as Greenlaw and Mr. Hanford had been expounding the rich significance of Milton's thought, and Saurat's book of 1925 gave wider currency to the new conception of Milton as a bold son of the Renaissance rather than a rigid son of the Reformation, a humanist rather than a grim Puritan. It was desirable that the pendulum should swing in that direction, even if it went too far. But we are concerned only with Saurat's use of biographical evidence, and may take account of what appear to be some fundamental aberrations.

In the first place Saurat sees Milton as above all a great heretic and proud independent rebel. Hence the poet of *Paradise Lost,* even though he condemns Satan, "pours out his own feelings" into the rebellious archangel, who is part not only of his own character but of his own mind. To take that view—which has, of course, in some form or other been the common post-Romantic view—is to make nonsense of the poem. One might as well say that Shakespeare poured his own feelings into Iago and Edmund and Macbeth.

Secondly, Saurat made Milton's first marriage the focal point of his whole life and work—as, about the same time, critics were making Wordsworth's French affair the focal center of his life and work. In his marriage, according to Saurat, the chaste and prayerful Milton was carried away by his senses and soon recognized with pain and sorrow that he, the dedicated servant of God, had betrayed his spiritual self. And he never got over the shock of his experience, with the knowledge that it brought of the strength of masculine passion and of feminine allurements. Even Milton's monistic metaphysical ideas are said to start from this conflict.

Now we can justly infer that Milton found he had made a grievous mistake, and we may assume that in his as in any other marriage the senses had a natural share. It is possible that Saurat's account of the marriage and its consequences is an account of what happened. But the fact is that we do not have the evidence. And the chief trouble is not so much that Saurat turns biographical conjecture into biographical fact, but that he makes this conjecture the basis of much of his analysis of the later poems, *Paradise Lost* in particular. Mary Powell is the weak, frivolous, and seductive Eve, and Adam is the rational and religious Milton led astray by passion; and when Adam and Eve are reconciled, we witness the reunion of Milton and his wife. Again it is logically possible that Milton's early experience entered into the poem; but, in view of the traditional and universal interpretation of the fall, we might wonder in what respects Milton's would have been different if he had never married at all.

In a more general way Saurat's overemphasis on biography and sex leads him to distort the nature of

the temptation and of Milton's main theme. The poet
being what Saurat says he is, the temptation has to turn
on Adam's succumbing to sensual passion. It is true
that Adam sins against the dictates of religion and
reason because his love for Eve oversways his will; but
that is the essence of the traditional conception of the
fall. On the other hand, Saurat neglects the far more
elaborate treatment of the temptation of Eve. If we
read the poem with our own eyes, we can hardly miss
Milton's continual stress on the motive of irreligious
intellectual pride as opposed to religious humility.
Satan, who himself had fallen through pride, decides
to base his campaign on that; he will appeal to the ambitious craving for godlike knowledge. This is the motive of the dream he puts into Eve's mind, of his successful dialogue with her, of her soliloquies before and
after her sin, and of her persuasion of Adam. It is the
moral of Raphael's long discourse on astronomy, and it
is strongly reiterated in the most significant place, the
conclusion of the poem, where religious faith and love
and obedience are contrasted with merely scientific
and external knowledge. All this, a large part of Milton's central theme, Saurat passes by; such "obscurant-
ism" is of course incompatible with his view of Milton
the man and the thinker. Like too many critics, Saurat
does not take sufficient account of the effect upon Milton of advancing age, disillusionizing experience, and
deepening religious insight; for him the author of
Paradise Lost is still the bold pamphleteer. So too,
when Christ in *Paradise Regained* breaks out against
vain bookishness, Saurat cannot square the utterance

with his notion of the great heretical rationalist and has to find an explanation, a rather feeble one, in the poet's fatigue.

If, in this short paper, Saurat is given a kind of bad eminence, it is an indirect and partial acknowledgment of the stimulating value of his work. We could glance at many other examples, old and new, of the use of biographical evidence and find similar mixtures of sound and unsound results; but everyone can supply such examples for himself and I need not assemble a list. When, to sum up, we review a good deal of Miltonic criticism, scholarly as well as unscholarly, from Johnson to Saurat and Eliot, we may arrive at the tentative conclusion that biographical evidence *is* of the first importance for the study of Milton—that is, that we need to look into the biographies of his critics.

To come to the general aspects of the problem, I may say at once that I have no special revelation. I can offer only a small set of truisms. It may, I should think, be laid down as a theoretical axiom that, if a work of art is not a self-sufficient entity and does not make its essential impact without biographical aids, there is something wrong with it (unless, of course, it has a topical subject). Nobody, we may remember, knows more than a few meager facts about most of the Greek and Roman writers, but we do not for that reason assume that we are debarred from comprehending ancient literature. And if our general axiom holds (with some reservations to be noted in a moment), it ought to be especially true of Milton, who is recognized by friend and foe alike as the classical artist *par excel-*

lence in English poetry. The word "classical," to be sure, embraces a number of qualities, but near the center are impersonality and normality.

For the reservations, it is understood that our theoretical reader is capable of bringing the author's other writings, prose as well as verse, to bear upon a particular poem. Also, it is freely granted that biographical evidence, though not a direct factor in the aesthetic experience, may stimulate receptivity and thereby promote and enrich the experience. As I have said elsewhere, it is in itself a moving experience to follow and relive Milton's spiritual evolution, and any good teacher or critic will use biography, knowing, however, that the discussion of a poem as a document is a beginning and not an end. To make these last remarks is not, I think, to unsay the general axiom about a poem's self-sufficiency. If, theoretically, the fullest biographical knowledge is necessary for the comprehension of a poem, difficulties ensue. One large fact has been mentioned, our ignorance of Greek and Roman biography. In the present case, we should have to admit that only a handful of Milton specialists can understand Milton. Possibly we Milton specialists think so. But if we do, we must recognize that our undergraduate teaching of Milton is doomed to failure because of our students' meager knowledge, and, worse still, that we ourselves cannot understand the work of countless other authors of whose biographies we are not complete masters.

In other words, a poem of Milton's should yield pretty much its full significance to a reader who possesses a very few biographical facts. We might look at the greatest of the early poems, *Lycidas,* one of the supreme examples in all English poetry of impersonal art charged with personal emotion. Although Milton had no such reason as Tennyson to feel personal sorrow, and although his own past, present, and future are his theme, he is asking himself the question of *In Memoriam*: how can he believe in God's providential care of a world in which a virtuous and promising life is cut off, a life, moreover, dedicated to the church which God allows to be infested with hireling shepherds? The pastoral convention provides a dramatic mask and controlling pattern for the poet's surging emotions, and beneath the smooth surface the struggle with doubt goes on until it ends with religious affirmation and serenity. If we see and feel this struggle and resolution as we should, how much of our response, we may ask, depends upon biographical knowledge gained outside the poem? Is there anything except two facts, and supplementary facts at that—namely, that the poet had recoiled bitterly from the church for which he had been destined, and that he wrote the poem after five long years of hard and outwardly unprofitable study? Everything else, except a modicum of literary and historical knowledge, is given in the poem. Further, since there have been some intelligent readers who could see in *Lycidas* nothing but an academic exercise, we might ask what would be the remedy for them, saturation in biography or saturation in the poem?

Let us move on to what may be called the *Lycidas* of Milton's old age, *Samson Agonistes,* which constitutes the most obvious test case. We are all—except Mr. Leavis—aware that *Samson* is the one great drama in English on the Greek model, that it is packed with intense emotion of a more profound and complex kind than inspired *Lycidas*. The theme is the process of Samson's regeneration, his development, under successive temptations, away from self-centered pride and despair to selfless humility and renewed trust in God. For most readers, perhaps, the drama is the most completely alive of all Milton's major works. That is, its original aim and effect are communicated the most fully, with the least loss through altered times and ideas, the least necessity for historical and philosophical reconstructions. Like the dramas of Aeschylus and Sophocles, it poses a universal and timeless problem in universal terms.

At the same time, as everyone knows, it can be read as an intensely personal document. With our knowledge, we see Restoration England and John Milton in the whole picture of Israel subject to a godless race and of the great rebel and deliverer now blind, helpless, tortured by physical and mental pains, while the bodies of other leaders are a prey to dogs and fowls, unjust tribunals, and the ungrateful mob; in the condemnation of the oppressors' idolatry, levity, and *hybris;* and, some would say, in the hero's fatal marriage to a daughter of the enemy—since the ghost of Mary Powell gets around much more surprisingly than that of Hamlet's father.

But one cannot bring up this familiar parallelism without adding some equally obvious comments. One is that even in his grand testament Milton remains a classical artist who depersonalizes and generalizes his public and private emotions. Every single item that we can call personal is an essential item in the drama of the Hebrew hero and arouses the appropriate dramatic reaction. Further, if we ask what the early biographers tell us, we find pictures of a man who, despite gout and blindness and other troubles, enjoys a placid and cheerful old age, with music, books, meditation, and the company that his character and fame have drawn about him. The biographies do not in any real sense explain either the old poet's capacity for defiance of the Restoration government or his much-tried but invincible religious faith. What we know of the state of mind that gave birth to *Samson* we infer from his verse and his pre-Restoration prose. Finally, if what we infer about Milton's personal experience and outlook explains the bare fact that he was able to bring emotional exaltation and intensity to the story of Samson, it is not "autobiography" that chiefly affects us. If the drama did not in itself move us greatly, our biographical knowledge would not bring it to life. When we respond as we do to "Eyeless in Gaza at the Mill with slaves," is it because we are thinking of Milton himself? Suppose, for instance, that we could work out parallels between the experience of Aeschylus and that of Prometheus: would such parallels appreciably heighten our response to the Greek drama?

We have only touched on some central questions concerning *Lycidas, Paradise Lost,* and *Samson,* but if we had time to look at all of Milton's poems I think we should find that their effect does not depend upon biographical information. From beginning to end, Milton's "self-expression" was objectified, generalized, and controlled by the dynamic principle of "decorum." Even in what appear to be the directly personal invocations of *Paradise Lost,* as C. S. Lewis has remarked, Milton is not speaking as a particular individual but is rather dramatizing himself as "the Christian poet" or "the blind poet." It is clearly essential to our full appreciation of the early poems that we should know something of the young idealist's situation and temper. It is also essential to our full appreciation of the major poems that we should realize what has happened to the young idealist, what these late works represent in their author's spiritual evolution: that the militant and confident revolutionist has lost his faith in mass movements, that he has been driven back to his impregnable inner fortress, that he has learned upon his pulses that "In His will is our peace." But all the essential knowledge we get from the works themselves, with help from Milton's other writings, not from biography. If we simply read *Paradise Lost* without prepossessions, its central import is fairly plain. Of course the more we know of literature, philosophy, and theology, the fuller our understanding, but that is a different affair—and the use of that kind of evidence and illustration, like the use of biography, can yield biased results. Even our glance at *Paradise Lost,* which is of course the crux of Miltonic interpretation, would suggest that critical deficiencies and aberrations have been largely caused by the use of biographical evidence. The critic's conscious or unconscious endeavor has often been not to study the poem itself, but to fit the poem into his picture of the man; hence the distortions in regard to rebellious pride, sensuality, Puritanism, and what not. We might conclude, then, that biographical evidence, as commonly used, has been as much of a hindrance as a help; but that, in the hands of ideally tactful and judicious scholar-critics (such as you and I), it can and should be useful in recreating the circumstances of composition, in promoting a receptive attitude, and perhaps now and then in throwing light on the text. Since Milton's poetry has suffered not only from recent prejudices in poetical taste but from prejudice against the man, the Miltonic scholar may well consider it part of his mission to establish a right view of the man. But that, however desirable, is only wiping spots off the spectacles with which we read the poetry.[3]

[3] While reading the proof of this paper I received from a student in my Milton course an amiable letter in which he said that he was left, above all, "with an appreciation of Milton as a human being, a fact which seems to me to be vital to an understanding of his work." This intelligent young Miltonist's emphasis made me wonder if there is a discrepancy between my preaching and my practice; but possibly it is covered by the reservations made in the paper.

Blake;
the Historical Approach

✻

By DAVID V. ERDMAN

I HAVE IMPOSED ON MYSELF . . . GROSSLY," wrote a schemer who had tried to impose on Blake but had mistaken his man, "I have imposed on myself . . . grossly in believing you to be one altogether abstracted from this world, holding converse with the world of spirits!" The mistake is common, but it is not exactly gross.

Blake himself encouraged it. "My abstract folly hurries me often away while I am at work," he told Thomas Butts, the muster clerk who bought his paintings, "carrying me over Mountains & Valleys, which are not Real, in a Land of Abstraction where Spectres of the Dead wander." A more straightforward person, or Blake in a more forthright record, might have said: I find it difficult to keep busy at this miniature portrait of Mrs. Butts,[1] because my mind wanders to the battlefield where men are dying, and then I see in my mind's eye the spirits of the contending powers.

We do not impose on ourselves if we believe that

[1] To be exact, Blake was occupied with other work for Butts when he wrote this letter; the miniature of Mrs. Butts was his chore the following year.

Blake held converse with the world of spirits, but we do if we think of either the poet or his spirits as "altogether abstracted from this world." As an observer of his own introspection, Blake understood the process of abstraction better than that; he knew that "it is impossible to think without images of somewhat [something] on this earth." At the age of twenty-six he saw Lunardi's first English demonstration of lighter-than-air craft (unless he was one of the few hapless Londoners who did not come out of their houses that day), and he knew that balloon navigators take some earth with them for ballast. When Blake soared, he did not expect to escape from the world of Bacon and Newton and Pitt, but to change its laws of gravity: "I . . . with my whole might chain my feet to the world of Duty & Reality," he explained; "but . . . the faster I bind, the better is the Ballast, for I, so far from being bound down, take the world with me in my flights."

We now understand this about Blake, in the sense that we recognize that he kept his sanity in spite of what he called "Nervous Fear" at the terrors of the times he lived in: "Fires inwrap the earthly globe," he wrote in 1793, "yet man is not consum'd." We may also understand it as a clue to his meaning, in the sense that Blake always kept his visions oriented in time and space, always knew where the sun was rising and what his horizons were. A person who wanted to escape the world altogether would not bother about horizons. But Blake never expected to get rid of his Urizen; he hoped only to teach him to be elastic and responsive as "the bound or outward circumference of

Energy"—he hoped only to change Urizen from a workmaster to a schoolmaster who would recognize his own limitations and never bind fast the infant "joys & desires." Blake did not like the *status quo,* but he loved England's green and pleasant land. He did not like the "turrets & towers & domes Whose smoke destroy'd the pleasant gardens, & whose running kennels Chok'd the bright rivers"; but his program was reconstruction, not emigration; he welcomed the "golden Builders" who were expanding London's suburbs. He stood "in London's darkness" when he wrote "of the building of Golgonooza, & of the terrors of Entuthon."

> I heard in Lambeth's shades.
> In Felpham I heard and saw the Visions of Albion.
> I write in South Molton Street what I both see and hear
> In regions of Humanity, in London's opening streets.

To William Blake, Time and Space were "Real Beings," and history was a very real, if "emblematic," texture.

II

The aim of the historical approach is to approximate Blake's own perspective, to locate, as nearly as we can, the moment and place in which he stood, to discover what he saw and heard in London's streets—what loomed on the horizon and what sounds filled the air.

The value of doing this for Blake's lyric poems may be open to question. For example, the "London" of *Songs of Experience* is a successful general symbol. In the lines

> In every voice, in every ban,
> The mind-forg'd manacles I hear,

everyone will agree that the phrase "mind-forg'd manacles" is an improvement in many ways over the rejected earlier wording, "german forged links." And
since we can do pretty well with the poem in contexts
of our own manufacture or out of our own experience,
some people will doubt the value of pursuing the clue
of the rejected reading, "german forged," to discover
that when Blake wrote the poem there was alarm
among freeborn Englishmen that German George, the
King of England, might be preparing to bring in "sub-
sidized Hessians and Hanoverians" "to cut the throats
of Englishmen," by way of following up the reiterated
royal "ban" or Proclamation against Seditious Writings, the intent of which was to put manacles on such
men as Paine and Blake. Nevertheless, the poem does
gain poignancy when read as a cry of anguish from
a city in the toils of antijacobinism. And our footnote
does at least discourage the assumption that Blake
meant to say that the victims of tyranny are victims
simply of manacles forged in their own minds. We
see that he was writing about thought control as well
as controlled thoughts.

Again, "The Tyger" is everyone's private possession
and an inexhaustible general symbol. Yet it is possible
for us to enlarge our view of its cosmic blacksmithery
by considering those points at which the images of
"The Tyger" touch the images of Blake's *French
Revolution* and *The Four Zoas*. In a synoptic vision of
the defeat of royal armies, as at Yorktown and at Valmy,

Blake says "the stars threw down their spears." At the climax of "The Tyger" he uses the same words. We can at least observe, if we wisely hesitate to draw conclusions, that Blake speaks of the vindication of the American and French revolutions in the same terms that he uses to suggest the vindication of the creation of the tiger.

In short, the *Songs of Experience* are well-nigh perfect crystals in themselves, and yet as critics of their essential force and brilliance—and of course as literary historians—we gain by knowing that they were created in the Year One of Equality, in the time of the birth of the French Republic and the London Corresponding Society.

The value of applying historical research to the avowedly prophetic and manifestly historical writings, on the other hand, should be beyond question. Yet not merely the difficulty of the task, but the sophisticated tradition through which Blake has come to us and which still directs our attention largely another way, have thus far prevented its being attempted in any thorough fashion.

Consider how the neglect of historical particulars impedes the progress of Professors Sloss and Wallis, the almost indefatigable editors of *William Blake's Prophetic Writings,* in their pursuit of the wandering Zoas. On the assumption that history and Blake's kind of "prophecy" are unrelated, they omit his *French Revolution* from their canon and with it many a passage that could shed light on later symbols. And when, in Blake's "long resounding, strong heroic verse," they come upon remarks about "War on the Rhine & Danube," they note in passing that Blake may be referring to the Napoleonic Wars. But these editors treat the wars of Urizen and Luvah as altogether abstract, for they have snipped off the clue thread that the poet provided when he said "Luvah is France" and they have neglected the trail that leads back from Urizen to George the Third, via the canceled plates of *America*. For example, at one point in *The Four Zoas,* near the end of Night I, aggressive Urizen, after having brooded "Eternal death to Luvah" and threatened a long war, suddenly reverses his field:

> But Urizen, with darkness overspreading all the armies,
> Sent round his heralds, secretly commanding to depart
> Into the north. Sudden, with thunder's sound, his multitudes
> Retreat from the fierce conflict . . .
> Mustering together in thick clouds, leaving the rage of Luvah
> To pour its fury on himself & on the Eternal Man.

"Points like this which do not explain themselves," say the editors, "can receive no light from without." I am afraid we must apply to the editors themselves, as well as to Urizen's armies, the lines which immediately follow: "Sudden down fell they all together into an unknown Space, Deep, horrible, without End."

This can happen to any of us on our way through *The Four Zoas,* and I do not mean to sound lofty. But the historical approach tells us that Night I contains a survey of the diplomatic and military relations between Britain and France up through 1799 and that at this point we have come to Britain's ill-fated Netherlands campaign, during which 36,000 men marched out and 20,000 marched back very precipitately, after fierce conflict, leaving the rage of Luvah or Napoleon to vent its fury on himself and on humanity ("the Eternal Man"). Napoleon was in a mood to do so, because he had just come through his coup of 18th Brumaire, which is described by Blake as a transformation of form from human to reptilian.[2]

I do not mean to imply that everything comes clear with the application of a little current history. In Blake's writings, as he has warned us, "there are many angles," and even the historical angle is never constant. The bard prefers to "walk up & down in 6,000 years," transposing furiously, translating the acts of Robespierre into those of Moses or abstracting the British heroes into their spiritual forms or telescoping together the Biblical and modern rebellions of slaves against Pharaohs in "dark Africa."

Sometimes we can understand a good deal of Blake's argument without paying much attention to his historical referents or even being aware of them. A great deal of Blake criticism, some of it very valuable in literary and philosophical insight, gets along famously in the swirling vortex of Blake's oratory without attending to what, in the narrowest literal sense, he is

[2] According to Linnell, by the way, Blake had an explanation from "some public man—ambassador, or something of the sort, that the Bonaparte of Italy was killed, and that another was somehow substituted from the exigent want of the name, who was the Bonaparte of the Empire." Alexander Gilchrist, *Life of William Blake,* Everyman's Library, London, 1945, p. 327. It is not clear whether Linnell or some other friend of Blake is being quoted.

talking about, or, to put the matter another way, without asking just precisely which historical persons or events have appeared to Blake as manifestations of eternal archetypes. The increasing interest in Blake's social thought, however, and in his excitement about the industrial revolution which did—and the social revolution which did not—take place while he was writing, now makes imperative the clearest possible definition of his minute particulars, especially of the dates and contexts of those works in which he deals with the history of his own times.

We speak loosely of all Blake's difficult works as "prophetic," yet in so figurative a sense that it is not customary to look for any literal message for the times —even in those two poems he himself called prophecies: *America, a Prophecy, 1793,* and *Europe, a Prophecy, 1794.* Yet Blake defined the nature of prophecy quite literally as an honest man's warning that "if you go on So, the result is So." And the warning of *America* is plain enough: that if kings such as Albion's Prince repeat against the Republic of France, in 1793, the crusade that failed against the Republic of America, they will reach the end of their rule over the people, who are "the strong."

The warning of *Europe,* in 1794, is more veiled and less specific in its prediction. But in its own language it is directed to Pitt and Parliament. It traces the steps leading to Britain's declaration of war in February, 1793, and describes the effect of the "gagging acts" of the following year. And its warning is that the trumpet of British power has marked the end of all royal power, for the war now raging is Armageddon, and the bloody sun now rising in France is the light of Christ's Second Coming. The peaceful child of 1789 seemed easy to wrap in swaddling clothes, but the "terrible Orc" of the embattled Republic will brook no counterrevolutionary attempt to crucify him. "The bloodthirsty people across the water," as Blake put it crudely in his notebook, "Will not submit to gibbet & halter."

If this interpretation can be demonstrated (and I believe that my chapter which does so is pretty securely based), how is it possible that with only one exception that I know of (Jacob Bronowski) critics have mistaken the obviously historical part of *Europe, a Prophecy* for a summary of events leading up to the French Revolution of 1789, a matter scarcely prophetic in any immediate sense? The answer is partly that even Mr. Schorer, with all his interest in the social theme, has been so busy dispelling the fogs of mysticism around Blake that he has left it to those who follow to explore the cleared ground. A more implicit difficulty is the fog in Blake's style itself. Nowhere is his private nomenclature more puzzling than in *Europe;* nowhere is there more sly shifting from one level of discourse to another, more difficulty with ambiguities of punctuation and sudden changes of pace. Yet once we have separated the central narrative from its mythological framework (which reaches from the morning of Christ's Nativity to the day of his Second Coming) we are dealing with an orderly sequence of events which can be fitted into the calendar of secular history as soon as we can date some of the minute particulars.

An example will illustrate the sort of detective work that can be done and that flows logically from the recognition that Blake's prophecy really deals with current events—and from an awareness that Blake, in dealing with current politics, is not altogether apart from the main stream of eighteenth-century political satire. Miss Miles has discovered a major source of Blake's language in the language of social satire. In a recent note in *The Art Quarterly* (Spring, 1949) I have called attention to Blake's use of themes in the political caricatures of James Gillray. In the text of *Europe* Blake describes a groveling "Guardian of the secret codes" in flight from Westminster Hall or the Houses of Parliament. He does not draw a picture of the incident, but in Gillray's caricatures there are two, "The Fall of the Wolsey of the Woolsack" and "Sin, Death and the Devil," published in May and June, 1792, which is acceptable as the year "before the trumpet blew" if we take the trumpet as Pitt's declaration of war against France. Both prints commemorate Pitt's ousting from his cabinet of the Lord High Chancellor Thurlow, Keeper of the Seal and Guardian of the King's Conscience. In the second print, which is a parody of Fuseli and of Milton, Thurlow is the Devil, Pitt is Death, and the Queen (for Pitt was a Queen's man at the time) is Sin, carrying the key to the backstairs and all our woe.[3]

[3] Here, too, is a key to Blake's emphasis in *Europe* on the cruelty of queens, pre-eminently the cruelty of the Queen of Heaven, who desires "That Woman, lovely Woman, may have dominion" through the code of "Sin," and who regards Rintrah (Pitt) as her knight-errant.

Pitt, who had been trying to rid himself of the formidable Thurlow for some time, found his opportunity when the chancellor ridiculed Pitt's Sinking Fund Bill as the work of "a mere reptile of a minister" and told Parliament that no bill should attempt to bind future governments. The grain of sedition in this remark must have seemed infinitesimal even in 1792. But Pitt, counting on his own indispensability at a time when he had filled the royal mind with constitutional alarm, asked the king to dismiss his Guardian, and the king obliged.

Blake treats the episode as a sign that the revolutionary world crisis has singed even the great Guardian of British law:

Above the rest the howl was heard from Westminster
        louder & louder;
The Guardian of the secret codes forsook his ancient
        mansion,
Driven out by the flames of Orc; his furr'd robes & false
        locks
Adhered and grew one with his flesh, and nerves & veins
        shot thro' them.
With dismal torment sick, hanging upon the wind, he
        fled
Groveling along Great George Street thro' the Park gate:
        all the soldiers
Fled from his sight: he drag'd his torments to the wilder-
        ness.

The "howl . . . louder & louder" of the judge driven out by the flames of rebellion may echo the "Irregular Ode" in the *Rolliad,* in which Thurlow on an earlier occasion is depicted as warning "every rebel soul" to tremble, as he grows "profane" with a "louder yet, and yet a louder strain."

Blake's particulars are unambiguous. The street that led from Westminster Hall, the mansion of the law, to St. James's Park was Great George Street. Blake's description of the chancellor in his dismal torment is as informed as the account in Thurlow's standard biography, where we read of his drive through the park to St. James's Palace to surrender the Seal, his dejection as "a solitary outcast," and his "diminished consequence" when seen "without his robes, without his great wig." There is no mistaking Blake's allusion to this unique event. In the whole span of time his poem might conceivably allude to, the only ermined justice driven out of Westminster was Baron Thurlow. Sloss and Wallis, it is true, conjectured that "this passage may be a reference to the London riots of . . . 1780, when the mob . . . burned Lord Mansfield's house." But this was poor guesswork. A simple check discloses that Mansfield's house was nowhere near Westminster or Great George Street or any park and that none of the fires of 1780 was in Westminster. This guess, missing the date by twelve years, demonstrates both the haphazard nature of Blake research when it has been a matter of seeking him in the material world and the sort of misleading commentary that still hedges Blake's historical clues from sight.

Much more is at stake, of course, than the right reading of a few historical allusions. Only when the central historical theme of *Europe* is cleared of misconceptions can we bring into focus the symbolism of the "Preludium" and of the mythological framework that encloses the central narrative, and only then can we see and properly appreciate the subtle use of Miltonic allusions there—and the architectural brilliance of the whole poem. But these are not matters for a hasty exposition.

In my book I shall show that a similar bringing into focus is possible for Blake's three epics, *The Four Zoas, Milton,* and *Jerusalem,* although these are not dated prophecies of the same sort as *America* and *Europe.*

III

I have been dwelling on the importance of the historical approach, and thus far my examples have been largely in the category of "light from without." For the rest of my time I want to talk about a method of reading Blake's "Visionary or Imaginative" language for clues or "Ulro Visions" which he himself supplies— for visions, that is, of the ultimate material starting-points of his visions. This method may be described as the reduction of Blake's fourfold vision to single vision. This is what I do when I say Rintrah "is" William Pitt, or Albion "is" the people of England. It is what Blake does when he says, "Luvah is France." So long as we recognize that we are dealing with only one side of Blake's fourfold, it is legitimate to do this— especially since the other sides are incomplete without this one, which is the ballast that keeps his balloon navigable.

I am well aware that Blake, in his impatience with

people who would see only with the eye and attend only to the ballast and not the flight, asserted "for My Self that I do not behold the outward Creation & that to me it is hindrance . . . it is as the dirt upon my feet." But to a detective or "Watch Fiend" like the historical scholar, the dirt upon Blake's feet is a good clue: it tells us where he has been walking. (Most of it upon Blake's feet is that gray clay known locally as "London stone.") You are familiar with the rest of the passage:

"When the Sun rises, do you not see a round disk of fire somewhat like a Guinea?" O no, no, I see an Innumerable company of the heavenly host crying, "Holy, Holy, Holy is the Lord God Almighty!" I question not my Corporeal . . . Eye. . . . I look thro' it & not with it.

Read backward, as I am suggesting for purposes of orientation, Blake's vision of an innumerable company singing Holy Holy "is" a sunrise.

When Blake writes to Flaxman, "The kingdoms of this World are now become the Kingdoms of God & His Christ, & we shall reign with him for ever & ever. The reign of Literature & the Arts commences," he is responding to rumors of peace between the kingdoms of France and Britain *just as he responded to the sunrise* (I quote a letter of October, 1801, but he used almost the same language at similar news a year earlier). Toward the end of the same letter he states more simply the hope "that France & England will henceforth be as One Country and their Arts One" and that he can soon go to Paris "to see the Great Works of Art." This simple and profound hope underlies much of the yearning in Blake's prophecies for an end to "the war of swords" or "corporeal war" and a commencement of the time of "intellectual war" when "sweet Science reigns." We impose on ourselves—yes, grossly—if we neglect the connection here between vision and history.

My point about method is that we can often work back from vision to starting-point if we but grant that the vision has a starting-point, is a vision "of" something. To Dr. Trusler, who told Blake "Your Fancy . . . seems to be in the other world, or the World of Spirits," Blake retorted: "I see Every thing I paint In This World, but Everybody does not see alike." Sometimes Blake's way of seeing what he paints is curiously close to the ways of Erasmus Darwin.

Fuseli, introducing Blake's designs to an orthodox audience, called attention to a quality of "taste, simplicity, and elegance" in Blake's "wildness." Miss Miles tells us that the major materials of Blake's language are those of mid-eighteenth-century poetry. And she makes the salutary observation that many of Blake's language habits which may have seemed unique are properly defined as *extensions* of eighteenth-century practice. With regard to some of the obscurities of Blake's figurative language, I suggest that they will often yield up their literal meanings when we approach them as the product of an exuberant *extension* of eighteenth-century practice in ornamental periphrasis, or Poetic Diction.

·Blake enjoyed referring, in a letter, to his wife's ocean bathing as "courting Neptune for an Embrace." In his poems he liked to refer to the ear as "the Gate of the Tongue." And he liked to take away the scaffolding of his conceit, too: he crossed out manuscript readings which made it clear that by the tongue's gate he meant the "auricular nerves." The gate of my tongue is your ear, your "auricular nerves," ultimately your reason; it is not simply what my nerves do that makes my speech incoherent, but the effect of the closing up of your inlets of soul. Urizen is your reason, not mine. In *The Four Zoas* a kind of Della Cruscan periphrasis is used in descriptions of battle. An iron gun is a "black bow" which shoots "darts of hail" or "arrows black." A smoking gun is a "cloudy bow." A cavalry charge under cover of artillery fire comes out like this: "Spur, spur your clouds Of death! . . . Now give the charge! bravely obscur'd With darts of wintry hail! Again the black bow draw!" The one who fires the first shot is the one who doth "first the black bow draw." When a Zoa and his Emanation are separated by the mischance of war, they do not say "Farewell for the duration," but, "Return, O Wanderer, when the day of Clouds is o'er."

In Blake's day the newspapers still referred to British soldiers as "the sons of Albion," and so does Blake. Often the Sons and Daughters of Albion represent the various institutions and vocations of English men and women. When the Daughters are at their "Needlework" they represent the textile trades. They strip wool ("Jerusalem's curtains") from sheep ("mild demons of the hills"), and the cellars and garrets where they work are "the dungeons of Babylon." When Blake walks about London "among Albion's rocks & preci-

pices" and looks into Albion's "caves of solitude & dark
despair," he is walking through the narrow cobbled
streets and looking into dark shops and tiny hovels—
"the caves of despair & death" in "the interiors of
Albion's Bosom." In the neoclassical tradition employed by Darwin, labor is done by gnomes and
nymphs. In Blake it is done by demons and spectres.
When young men and women enter apprentice slavery
or the army, they are "taking the spectral form." Blake
the journeyman engraver is the "spectre" of Blake the
poet.

For a concentrated exercise in this materialistic
method of reading Blake's "emblematic texture," let
us study some of the passages in which Blake is looking
at himself at work, engraving or etching on polished
copper plates with engraving tools or with varnish
and nitric acid (aqua fortis). Here the material referents are palpable, and the differences between matter
and manner stand out plain.

Blake's best known reference to the etching process,
which he employed in all his "Illuminated Printing,"
is found in *The Marriage of Heaven & Hell.*

On the abyss of the five senses, where a flat sided steep
frowns over the present world, I saw a mighty Devil
folded in black clouds, hovering on the sides of the rock.
With corroding fires he wrote the following sentence now
perceived by the minds of men, & read by them on earth.

The abyss into which Blake is looking is the mirror-
like surface of his copper plate. When he focuses on
the surface itself, he sees a flat sided rock. When he
looks into the mirror world and orients toward *that* as

real, then the "present world" is beneath it, and the flat surface is a steep cliff overhanging the present world. The mighty Devil folded in black clouds and hovering on the sides of the rock is the mirror image of Blake in his black suit pouring aqua fortis ("corroding fires") onto the copper to destroy the abyss except where he has written with impermeable ink or varnish.[4] His sentence, appearing on the plate in reverse, is only perceived by the minds of men when it is printed and reversed back from the abysmal state. The relationship between the mirror image and the direct image symbolizes the relationship between the vision conveyed to "minds" and the physical sentence on the copper. Thus a full understanding of this passage depends on—or begins with—our visualizing the rudiments of the process: once we "see" that, we can proceed to explore the further connotations of "the abyss of the five senses." [5]

For the process of line engraving we may turn to *The Four Zoas,* where we will find a Spectre who "drave his solid rocks before Upon the tide." The tide is the pond-like surface of the plate, upon which the engraving Spectre lodges the bits of copper gouged out by the graver as he pushes it forward with his hand —driving "his solid rocks before Upon the tide." Here again is the abyss which is not an abyss, the apparently solid surface which opens to infinite meaning—repre-

[4] In conventional intaglio etching the plate would be covered with a blackened ground, but for his relief etching Blake worked directly on the polished surface.
[5] I say the rudiments of the process. Notice that Blake keeps secret his actual method of getting words onto the plate.

sented by an apparently non-solid tide or abyss which
supports rocks or a rock.

The pushing of the graver (or etching needle) makes
channels for the ink, and since these channels are technically called furrows, the most obvious metaphor is
that of plowing. The complaint that the poet's children
have been "plow'd and harrow'd" for another's profit
is a complaint that Blake's drawings have been engraved (and etched) by Schiavonetti for his profit.[6] All
the plowing mentioned in the prophetic works is not
engraving, of course. But sometimes even the direct
description of agriculture contains an implied comparison to the poet's own manner of earning his bread.

Wisdom is sold in the desolate market where none come
    to buy,
And in the wither'd field where the farmer plows for
    bread in vain.

Blake had English famine years in mind when he wrote
this. But he had also recently plowed for bread in vain,
metaphorically, in the sense that he had engraved
forty-three plates for an edition of Young's *Night
Thoughts* which none had come to buy.

But let us turn to a passage where the focus is, both
literally and metaphorically, on the plowing which is
engraving. Here the "weeping" of "clods" in "the
plowed furrow" suggests that Blake, like his fellow
craftsmen, is resorting to "the engraver's best auxiliary,
aquafortis," [7] which makes the bits of copper dissolve.

[6] Schiavonetti's "etchings" for *The Grave* combined intaglio etching
and engraving, while much "line engraving," including Blake's
journeywork, employed intaglio etching for foliage and background.
[7] Some people "imagine that the curves, lines, hatchings . . . in a

And the "many" who speak are, according to the context, the multiple eyes of God, that is, of Blake's imagination. "Many conversed on these things as they labour'd at the furrows," says Blake, meaning that many ideas occurred to him as his eyes and imagination attended to the lines he was engraving.

The passage I have begun to quote, *Jerusalem* 55, contains another reminder that these material aspects of Blake's meaning are but the dirt on his feet, or, as he puts it here, but

as the moss upon the tree, or *dust upon the plow,*
Or as the sweat upon the labouring shoulder, or as the chaff
Of the wheat-floor or as the dregs of the sweet wine-press.
Such are these Ulro Visions: for tho' we sit down

—"we" are the Eyes speaking about themselves, "the Human Organs" who can at will contract "into Worms or Expand . . . into Gods,"—

for tho' we sit down within
The plowed furrow, list'ning to the weeping clods till we
Contract or Expand Space at will; or if we raise ourselves
Upon the chariots of the morning, Contracting or Expanding Time,
Every one knows, we are One Family, One Man blessed for ever.

Blake is speaking about the unity of life in the Imagination which denies the limitations and divisions

---

line engraving are produced by a slow and laborious operation . . . . but the hard manual work involved in the production of the furrows or ditches in the metal, has been almost entirely superseded, since the days of Albert Dürer . . . by the use of the engraver's best auxiliary, aquafortis." Andrew Tuer, *Bartolozzi and His Works*, London, 1881, I, 80.

accepted by the eyes that see only matter. But our concern at the moment is with the dust and the sweat. What the eyes say is this: We may focus on the furrow being engraved, until we look through that and see a world in a grain of copper; or we may look out the window and in imagination follow the sun ("raise ourselves Upon the chariots of the morning") until we see past, present, and future Time. In that way we see the unity of all space and all time.

Through the wrong end of the telescope we (I mean you and I, now) can see William Blake, sweating at "the meer drudgery" of engraving, and accomplishing "not one half of what I intend, because my Abstract folly hurries me often away while I am at work."

The difference between engraving and relief etching, we must understand, represented the difference between the hack work Blake had to do for a living and the prophetic work he did "to lay up treasures in heaven" and as a soldier of the imagination. His Spectre did most of the plowing and could boast that his labor was necessary to put a world "underneath the feet of Los" and bring a smile of hope to "his dolorous shadow" of a wife. Many a time, declared the surly Spectre, his engraving kept them all from "rotting upon the Rocks" and put "spungy marrow" into the prophet's "splinter'd bones." Yet Blake longed to rise above the "meer drudgery" of engraving, longed to escape this Spectre's power and cast him "into the Lake," perhaps into the very tide upon which he drave his solid rocks.

The writing and etching of his own poems, on the

other hand, was done by Los, bard and prophet, "without Fatigue." With corrosive fires he burnt apparent surfaces away to reveal the "eternal lineaments" of truth.[8] Or he would "pour aqua fortis on the Name of the Wicked & turn it into an Ornament & an Example." Or, in his favorite imagery, he would forge "under his heavy hand the hours, The days & years" of Tyranny, and thus bind the wicked "in chains of iron."

This shift of image from etcher to blacksmith, from worker with acid on copper to worker with iron and steel in fire, was essential for the connotations of cosmic bardic power. In "The Tyger" Blake could scarcely have written: What the hand dare seize the acid-bottle? An engraver's shop did have a small anvil for leveling, and a hand-bellows for drying, copper plates. But the blacksmith's mighty hammer, anvil, tongs, chain, and furnaces of intellectual war were far more effectual equipment for a bard in competition with the dark Satanic mills which were producing "ramm'd combustibles" and "molten metals cast in hollow globes, & bored Tubes in petrific steel" (Wilkinson's new process for making cannon barrels was to bore them from solid cast steel). There was also the emotional identification with the working artisan rather than with the more isolated intellectual worker, who might talk about books and pen and paper. Los, as

[8] I suppose we may look upon Blake's reading of the Bible in the infernal sense as a heretical blossom of that medieval exegetical tradition according to which, as Mr. Robertson has pointed out, the aim of the wise man is to cut away the *cortex* or *integumentum* and reveal the nucleus of inner meaning. The tradition reaches Blake, of course, by way of the Protestant mystics and euhemerist antiquaries.

blacksmith, could quite legitimately "wipe the sweat from his red brow." Ultimately Blake pictured him as assisted by a thousand laboring sons, because Blake knew that a multitude of furnaces and fellow laborers, a whole intellectual movement, would be needed to build the new Jerusalem, when free men, "Young Men of the New Age," inherited "the Ruin'd Furnaces of Urizen."

Another strong symbol of effective energy is the printing press, especially in its apocalyptic analogue, the human wine press "call'd War on Earth." The figure of the printer, however, does not compare in power to that of the blacksmith. In the preface to *Jerusalem* Blake prays in humble fashion that his own "types" shall not be "vain." But only once, in *Milton,* is the press of Los specifically called a "Printing-Press," and even there our attention is quickly shifted to a fiercer image. As the poet "lays his words in order above the mortal brain," his types are compared to the steel teeth of a cogwheel which "turn the cogs of the adverse wheel."

At one point in *Jerusalem* Blake does speak of the publication of paper books, when he refers to the pages of a pamphlet against war as "leaves of the Tree of Life." But here he is referring, not to his own fire-seared labors, which he expects to have read only by "future generations," but to the milder and more ephemeral publications of men "scarcely articulate."

In the passage I refer to (*Jerusalem* 45–46), a considerable speech or sermon by someone called "Bath" is spoken of as a sheaf of pages and handed to someone called "Oxford, immortal Bard" with a request that Oxford write an introduction to the public—or so I interpret the following: "Oxford, take thou these leaves of the Tree of Life; with eloquence That thy immortal tongue inspires, present them to Albion: Perhaps he may receive them, offer'd from thy loved hands." Here is a pretty concrete situation, and it ought certainly to yield up its literal meaning to an assiduous Watch Fiend. Both prongs of our historical method must be employed. On the one hand we must establish the historical context of *Jerusalem* by pinning down various kinds of internal evidence. This I have done fairly thoroughly and have found that *Jerusalem* deals with the latter phase of the Napoleonic wars and that the poem's central prophetic theme is a plea to Albion and his Sons not to pursue the war with France to mutual ruin or to make a vengeful peace that would destroy the freedom and national brotherhood of the two nations. On the eve of Waterloo the latter probability weighs on Blake's mind: "What can I do to hinder the Sons of Albion from taking vengeance? or how shall I them perswade?" In the earlier speech by Bath, he fears for Albion's own destruction.

We must on the other hand examine Blake's hyperbole to see what kind of literal statement the eloquence of Bath and Oxford can be reduced to. Translated into ordinary language, Bath's speech is an anti-war tract addressed to the people of England ("O Albion") alluding to the abolition of the slave trade, a Parliamentary measure enacted in 1807, and inveighing against imperial selfhood or British national pride: "however high Our palaces and cities and however fruitful are our fields, In Selfhood we are nothing." The remark that Bath speaks "in midst of Poetic Fervor" suggests that the author of the tract has been currently engaged in writing verse, and the statement that Bath is one who "first assimilated with Luvah in Albion's mountains" means, within the framework of date and theme established for *Jerusalem*, that he was one of the first British intellectuals to preach peace with France in the present period, that is, since the renewal of war in 1803.

Armed with these clues, my assistant, Martin Nurmi, soon found the preacher-poet of Bath by looking into a bibliography of works written in that city. In 1808, shortly after the passage of the Abolition Bill, the Reverend Richard Warner published *A Letter to the People of England: on Petitioning the Throne for the Restoration of Peace*. In the same year he published such evidence of "Poetic Fervor" as *Bath Characters* and *Rebellion in Bath, an Heroico-Odico-Tragico-Comico Poem*. As for Warner's being one who "first assimilated with Luvah," in 1804 he startled Bath and London with the publication of a fast-day sermon entitled *War Inconsistent with Christianity*, which advocated that Englishmen refuse to bear arms even in case of an invasion by Napoleon. Reviewed widely and heatedly, Warner's sermon went into four editions within a few months and continued to be reissued throughout the war. In *Bath Characters* Warner caricatures himself thus:

Dick preaches foul DEMOCRACY;
And forces luckless loyal sinners,
To hear his rant, and spoil their dinners

—or so his foes say. But "On the *broad basis*" he'll rely "Of GENUINE CHRISTIANITY."

"Stripped of its Oriental dress," says Warner in his Fast Sermon, "the declaration of CHRIST may fairly be taken as a direct and unequivocal reprehension of hostile violence, both in individuals and states." "However brilliant the successes are with which their arms shall be crowned; whatever acquisitions of territory conquest may unite to their ancient empire . . . WAR is the GREATEST CURSE with which a nation can be afflicted, and . . . all its imaginary present advantages, or future contingent benefits, are but as 'dust in the balance,' and as 'chaff before the wind.' " Warner's sentiments are undoubtedly those of Blake's "voice of Bath."

In his 1808 *Letter to the People* Warner's alarm that the "national spirit . . . is graduating into a spirit of lawless ambition, and aggressive violence" parallels Bath's concern lest Albion should "slay Jerusalem in his fearful jealousy," and on the other hand his warning, "Be *expeditious* . . . lest the concluding scene of the war be performed upon your own shores; lest [Britain's] peaceful plains exhibit those horrors which the nations of the continent have so long and so largely experienced," suggests the tenor of Bath's urgency: "his [Albion's] death is coming apace . . . for alas, we none can know How soon his lot [the lot of Jesus or of Luvah-France] may be our own."

None of the Warner pamphlets I have seen discusses
the slave trade, although in the *Letter* a passing reference to the "deliverers of Africa, the friends of the
poor," may have been enough to prompt Bath's lines.
Nor have I yet encountered—though I do not despair
of doing so [9]—any of Warner's "leaves" with an introduction by an Oxford poet saying, "In mild perswa-
sion," something like this:

Thou art in Error, Albion, [in] the Land of Ulro. . . .
Reason not on both sides. Repose upon our bosoms.

[9] I have still (in 1963) not found a pamphlet introduced by "Oxford"; perhaps Blake's friend "Edward, the bard of Oxford," was
simply handing out copies of Warner's pamphlet with appropriate
verbal comment.

Wordsworth's "Ode: Intimations of Immortality"

✹

By LIONEL TRILLING

CRITICISM, we know, must always be concerned with
the poem itself. But a poem does not always exist
only in itself; sometimes it has a very lively existence
in its false or partial appearances. Criticism must take
these simulacra into account; and sometimes, in its effort to come at the poem as it really is, criticism does
well to allow the simulacra to dictate at least its opening moves. In speaking about the "Ode: Intimations
of Immortality from Recollections of Early Childhood," I should like to begin by considering an interpretation of the poem which is now widespread.
According to this interpretation, the "Ode" is—I
quote Dean Sperry's statement of a view held by
many other admirable critics—"Wordsworth's conscious farewell to his art, a dirge sung over his departing powers."

How did this interpretation—erroneous, as I believe—come into being? Although the "Ode" may be
quoted to substantiate it, I do not think it has been

drawn directly from the poem itself. To be sure, the
"Ode" is not wholly perspicuous: Wordsworth himself seems to have thought it difficult, and in the Fen-
wick notes he speaks of the need for competence and
attention in the reader. The difficulty does not lie in
the diction, which is simple, or even in the syntax,
though that is obscure, but in contradictory statements
within the poem itself and in the ambiguity of some
of its crucial words. Yet the erroneous interpretation
I am dealing with seems to me to arise not from any
intrinsic difficulty but, rather, from certain extraneous
and unexpressed assumptions about the nature of the
mind.

We are very much aware nowadays that such tacit
assumptions lie hidden deep below what we say of all
poetry. Usually it is only with great effort that we can
bring them to consciousness. But in speaking of Wordsworth one of the commonest of our unexpressed ideas
comes so close to the surface of our thought that it
needs only to be grasped and named. I refer to the
belief that poetry is made by means of a particular
poetic faculty—a faculty which may be isolated and
defined.

It is this belief, based wholly upon assumption,
which underlies all the speculations of the critics who
attempt to explain Wordsworth's poetic decline by
one or another of the events of his life. And in effect
such an explanation is a way of *defining* Wordsworth's
poetic faculty. For what the biographical critics are
telling us is that Wordsworth wrote great poetry by

means of a faculty which depended upon his relations with Annette Vallon; or by a faculty which operated only so long as he admired the French Revolution; or by a faculty which flourished by virtue of a particular pitch of youthful sense-perception; or by virtue of a certain attitude toward Jeffrey's criticism; or by virtue of a certain relation with Coleridge.

Now, no one can reasonably object to the idea of mental determination in general, and I do not intend to make out that poetry is an unconditioned activity. Still, this particular notion of mental determination which implies that Wordsworth's poetical genius failed when it was deprived of some single emotional circumstance is so much too simple and so much too mechanical that I think we must inevitably reject it. Certainly what we know of poetry does not allow us to refer it to any single faculty. Nothing less than the whole mind, the whole man, will suffice for its origin. And such was Wordsworth's own view of the matter.

But there is another unconscious and unsubstantiated assumption at work in the common biographical interpretation of the "Ode"—the belief that there is a natural and inevitable warfare between the poetic faculty and the philosophic faculty. Wordsworth himself did not believe in this antagonism—indeed, he held an almost contrary view—but Coleridge thought that philosophy had encroached upon and destroyed his own powers, and the critics who speculate on Wordsworth's artistic fate seem to prefer Coleridge's psychology to Wordsworth's own. Observing in the

"Immortality Ode" a contrast between something called "the visionary gleam" and something called "the philosophic mind," they leap to the conclusion that the "Ode" is Wordsworth's conscious farewell to his art, a dirge sung over departing powers.

Well, I am so far from agreeing with this conclusion that I believe the "Ode" is not only not a dirge but actually a dedication to new powers. Wordsworth did not, to be sure, realize his great hopes for these powers, but that is quite another matter.

As with many poems, it is hard to understand any part of the "Ode" until we first understand the whole of it. I will therefore say at once what I think the poem is chiefly about. It is a poem about growing; some say it is a poem about growing old, but I believe it is about growing up. It is incidentally a poem about optics and then, inevitably, about epistemology. It is concerned with ways of seeing and then with ways of knowing and ultimately with ways of acting. For, as usual with Wordsworth, knowledge implies liberty and power. In only a limited sense is the "Ode" a poem about immortality.

Both formally and historically the poem is divided into two main parts. The first part, consisting of four stanzas, states an optical phenomenon and asks a question about it. The second part, stanzas v–xi, answers that question and is itself divided into two parts, the first despairing, the second hopeful. Some years separate the composition of the question from that of the answer; the poet himself says that the interval was at least two years—actually it was no less than four.

The question of the first part is this:

> Whither is fled the visionary gleam?
> Where is it now, the glory and the dream?

All the first part leads to this question, but although it moves in only one direction it takes its way through more than one mood. The climax of the question is effective by reason of the number of moods it resolves; there are at least three moods before the question is asked.

The statement the first stanza makes is relatively simple. "There was a time" when all common things seemed clothed in "celestial light," when they had "the glory and the freshness of a dream." In a poem presumably about immortality we ought perhaps pause over the word "celestial," but the present elaborate title was not given the poem until much later, and conceivably at the time of writing the first part the idea of immortality was not in Wordsworth's mind. Celestial light probably means only something different from ordinary, earthly, scientific light; it is a light of the mind, shining even in darkness—"by night or day"—and is perhaps similar to the light which is praised in the invocation to the third book of *Paradise Lost*.

The second stanza goes on to develop this first mood, speaking of the ordinary, physical kind of vision and suggesting further the meaning of "celestial." We must remark that in this stanza Wordsworth, so far from observing a diminution of his physical senses, actually affirms their strength; he is at pains to tell us how vividly he sees the rainbow, the rose, the moon, the stars, the water, the sunshine. I emphasize this because some of those who find the "Ode" a dirge for the poetic power maintain that the power failed with the failure of Wordsworth's senses at the age of thirty-two. We might observe here, as others have observed elsewhere, that though Wordsworth had acute senses he never did have the special and perhaps modern sensibility of his sister or of Coleridge, who are so aware of exquisite particularities; his finest passages are moral, emotional, subjective, and whatever visual intensity they have comes from his response, not from his observation.

And not only does Wordsworth confirm his senses, but he also confirms his ability to perceive beauty; he tells us how he responds to the loveliness of the rose and of the stars reflected in the water; he can deal, in the way of Fancy, with the delight of the moon when there are no competing stars in the sky, can see in Nature certain moral properties, finding the sunshine a "glorious birth." But here he pauses to draw distinctions from that fascinating word "glory": despite his perception of the glory of the sunshine, he knows "That there hath past away a glory from the earth."

And now, with the third stanza, the poem begins to complicate itself. It is *while* Wordsworth is aware of the "optical" change in himself, the loss of "glory," that there comes to him "a thought of grief." The word "while," that is, must be taken to mean that for some time he had been conscious of the "optical" change *without* feeling grief; the grief, then, would seem to be coincidental with, but not necessarily caused by, the change. And this grief is not of long duration, for we learn that

> A timely utterance gave that thought relief
> And I again am strong.

It would be not only interesting but also useful to know what that "timely utterance" was, and I should like to hazard a guess; but first I should like to follow the development of the "Ode" a little further.

Stanza iv goes on to tell us that the poet, after gaining relief from the "timely utterance," felt himself quite in harmony with the joy of nature in spring. The tone of this stanza is ecstatic, and twice there is a halting repetition of words to express a kind of painful intensity of response: "I feel—I feel it all" and "I hear, I hear, with joy I hear!" Wordsworth sees, hears, feels —and with that "joy" which both he and Coleridge felt to be so necessary to the poet. But despite the response, despite the joy, the ecstasy changes in a wonderful modulation to sadness:

> —But there's a Tree, of many, one,
> A single Field which I have looked upon,
> Both of them speak of something that is gone:
> The Pansy at my feet
> Doth the same tale repeat:

And what they utter is the question:

> Whither is fled the visionary gleam?
> Where is it now, the glory and the dream?

Now, the interpretation which makes the "Ode" a dirge over departing powers and a conscious farewell to art takes it for granted that the visionary gleam, the glory and the dream are the powers by which Wordsworth made poetry. This interpretation gives to the "Ode" a place in Wordsworth's life exactly analogous to the place that "Dejection: an Ode" had in Coleridge's life and not only relates the two poems but actually makes them symbiotic. That the two poems are very intimately connected is of course true, and Coleridge in his poem most certainly does say that his poetic powers are gone or going; he is very explicit, and the language he uses is very close to that of Wordsworth in the "Ode." He tells us that upon "the inanimate cold world" there must issue from the soul "a light, a glory, a fair luminous cloud" and that this glory *is* Joy, which he himself no longer possesses. Wordsworth, however, tells us that he has strength, that he has Joy, but still he has not the glory. In short, we have no reason to assume that when he asks the question at the end of the fourth stanza he means, "Where has my creative power gone?" Wordsworth tells us how he made poetry; he says he made it out of the experience of his senses as worked upon by his contemplative intellect; but he nowhere tells us that he made poetry out of visionary gleams, out of glories, or out of dreams.

To be sure he writes very often about gleams. The word "gleam" is a favorite one, and a glance at the Lane Cooper concordance will confirm our recollection that Wordsworth, whenever he has a moment of insight or happiness, talks about it in the language of light. His great poems are about moments of enlightenment; he uses "glory" in the abstract modern sense, but always with an awareness of the old concrete sense of a visible nimbus. But this momentary and special light is the subject matter of his poetry, not the power of making it. The moments are moments of understanding, but Wordsworth does not say that they make writing poetry any easier. Indeed, in lines 59–131 of the first book of *The Prelude* he expressly says that the moments of clarity are by no means always matched by poetic creativity.

As for dreams and poetry, there is some doubt about the meaning that Wordsworth gave to the word "dream" used as a metaphor. In "Expostulation and Reply" he seems to say that dreaming—"dream my time away"—is a good thing, but he is ironically using his interlocutor's deprecatory word, and he really does not mean "dream" at all. In the Peele Castle verses, which have so close a connection with the "Immortality Ode," he speaks of the "poet's dream" and makes it synonymous with "gleam," with "the light that never was, on sea or land," and with the "consecration." But the beauty of the famous lines often makes us forget to connect them with what follows, for Wordsworth says that gleam, light, consecration, and dream would have made an "illusion," or, in the 1807 version, a "delusion." Professor Beatty reminds us that in the 1820 version Wordsworth destroyed the beauty of the lines in order to make his intention quite clear; he wrote:

> and add a gleam
> Of lustre known to neither sea nor land,
> But borrowed from the youthful Poet's Dream.

That is, according to the terms of Wordsworth's conception of the three ages of man, the youthful Poet was, as he had a right to be, in the service of Fancy and therefore saw the sea as calm. But Wordsworth himself can no longer see in the way of Fancy; he has, he says, "submitted to a new control." This seems to be at once a loss and a gain. The loss: "A power is gone, which nothing can restore." The gain: "A deep distress hath humanised my Soul"; this is gain because happiness without "humanisation" "is to be pitied, for 'tis surely blind"; to be "housed in a dream" is to be "at distance from the kind." In the "Letter to Mathetes" he speaks of the Fancy as "dreaming"; and the Fancy is, we know, a lower form of intellect in Wordsworth's hierarchy, and peculiar to youth.

But though Wordsworth uses the word "dream" to mean illusion, we must remember that he thought illusions might be very useful. They often led him to proper attitudes and allowed him to deal successfully with reality. In *The Prelude* he tells us how his reading of fiction made him able to look at the face of a drowned man without too much horror; how a kind of superstitious conviction of his own powers was useful to him; how the mist-magnified bulk of the Shepherd stirred his thoughts to consider the majesty of man; and in *The Excursion* he is quite explicit about the salutary effects of superstition. But he was interested in dreams, not for their own sake, but for the sake of reality. Dreams may *perhaps* be associated with poetry, but reality *certainly* is; and reality for Wordsworth comes fullest with Imagination, which is the offspring of Reason, the faculty of Maturity. The loss of the "dream" may be painful, but it does not necessarily mean the end of poetry.

And now for a moment I should like to turn back to the "timely utterance," because I think an understanding of it will help get rid of the idea that Wordsworth was saying farewell to poetry. Professor Garrod believes that this "utterance" was "My Heart Leaps Up When I Behold," which was written the day before the "Ode" was begun; its theme, the legacy left by the child to the man, is a dominant theme of the "Ode," and its last lines are used as the epigraph to the "Ode." But I should like to suggest that the "utterance" was something else. In line 43 Wordsworth says, "Oh evil day! if I were sullen," and the word "sullen" leaps out at us as a striking and carefully chosen word. Now there is one poem in which Wordsworth says that he was sullen; it is "Resolution and Independence." [1]

[1] I follow Professor Garrod in assuming that the "utterance" was a poem; but of course it may have been a letter or a spoken word. And if indeed the "utterance" does refer to "Resolution and Independence" it may not refer to the poem itself but, as my friend

We know that Wordsworth was working on the first part of the "Ode" on the twenty-seventh of March, the day after the "Rainbow" poem. On the seventeenth of June he added a little to the "Ode," but what he added or where the addition was made, whether in the middle or at the end, we do not know. Between the two dates of the composition Wordsworth and Dorothy had paid a visit to Coleridge, who was sojourning at Keswick; during this visit Coleridge, on April 4, had written and Wordsworth had read "Dejection: an Ode." Coleridge's mental state was very bad (still, not so bad as to keep him from writing a great poem), and the Wordsworths were much distressed. A month later, on May 3, Wordsworth began to compose "The Leech-Gatherer," later known as "Resolution and Independence"; it is this poem that is, I think, the timely utterance. It is a poem about the fate of poets; also it is a poem about sullenness, the word being used in the same sense in which Dante used it when he described the people in the Fifth Circle who are submerged in the mire: " 'Sullen were we in the sweet air, that is gladdened by the sun, carrying lazy smoke within our hearts; now lie we sullen [2] here in the black mire!'

Jacques Barzun suggests to me, it may refer to what the Leech-gatherer in the poem says to the poet; certainly in the poem it is what the old man "utters" that gives the poet "relief." Still, it was not the actual historical "utterance" that gave the actual "relief"— it antedated the writing of the poem by two years—but rather its recollection and use in the poem: the old man's "utterance" becomes, in effect, Wordsworth's own.

[2] Dante's word is "tristi"; in "Resolution and Independence" Wordsworth speaks of "dim sadness."

This hymn they gurgle in their throats, for they cannot speak it in full words"—that is, they cannot now have relief by timely utterance, as they would not on earth. And "sullenness" I take to be the creation of difficulties where none exist, the working of a self-destroying imagination such as a modern mental physician would be quick to recognize as a neurotic symptom. Wordsworth's poem is about a sudden unmotivated anxiety after a mood of great exaltation; he speaks of this reversal of feeling as something experienced by himself before and known to all. In this mood he is the prey of "fears and fancies," of "dim sadness" and "blind thoughts." These feelings concern two things. One of them—natural enough in a man under the stress of approaching marriage, for Wordsworth was to be married in October—is economic destitution. He reproaches himself for his past indifference to the means of living and thinks of what may follow from this carefree life: "solitude, pain of heart, distress, and poverty." His black thoughts are led to the fate of poets "in their misery dead," among them Chatterton and Burns. The other concern is mental distress:

We Poets in our youth begin in gladness;
But thereof come in the end despondency and madness.

Coleridge, we must suppose, was in Wordsworth's thoughts, but he is of course thinking chiefly of himself. It is well known how the poem ends, how with some difficulty of utterance the poet brings himself to talk with an incredibly old leech-gatherer and, taking heart from the man's resolution and independence, becomes again "strong."

I do not think that this great poem should be given a crucial meaning in Wordsworth's life. It makes use of a mood to which everyone, certainly every creative person, is now and again a victim; and, as I have said, the poem was written at a time in Wordsworth's life when it was natural that he should conjure up difficulties.[3] I have tried to show that the poem is the timely utterance spoken of in the "Ode," not merely to gratify a scientific curiosity—for in a way it does not matter what the timely utterance was, enough for the poem that there was one—but because it is a very precise and hard-headed account of a mood of great fear and because it deals in a very explicit way with the dangers that beset the poetic life. But though Wordsworth urges himself on to think of all the bad things that can possibly happen to a poet and specifies solitude, pain of heart, distress, and poverty, cold, pain and labor, all fleshly ills, and even madness, he never says that a poet is in danger of losing his talent. Whether or not "Resolution and Independence" is the "timely utterance," it must have some biographical connection with the first part of the "Ode," having been written at the same time. It seems reasonable to suppose that if Wordsworth were saying farewell to his talent in the "Ode," there would be some hint of an endangered or

[3] The actual meeting with the leech-gatherer took place some two years before.

vanishing talent in the other poem. But there is none; at its end Wordsworth is resolute in poetry.

Must we not, then, look with considerable skepticism at such interpretations of the "Ode" as suppose without question that the "gleam," the "glory," and the "dream" constitute the power of making poetry?—especially when we remember that at a time still three years distant Wordsworth in *The Prelude* will speak of himself as becoming a *"creative* soul" (Bk. XII, line 207) despite the fact that, as he says (Bk. XII, line 281), he "sees by glimpses now."

The second half of the "Immortality Ode" is divided into two large movements, stanzas v–viii and stanzas ix–xi; both movements answer the question with which the first part ends. The two answers seem to contradict each other: the first issues in despair, the second in hope; the first uses a language strikingly supernatural, the second is precisely naturalistic. The two parts even differ in the statement of fact, for the first says that the gleam is gone, whereas the second says that it is not gone, but only transmuted. It is necessary to understand this contradiction, but not necessary to resolve it: from the circuit between its two poles comes the power of the poem.

The first of the two answers (stanzas v–viii) tells us where the visionary gleam has gone by telling us where it came from. It is a remnant of a preëxistence in which we enjoyed a way of seeing and knowing now quite gone from us. We come into the world, not with minds that are merely *tabulae rasae,* but with a kind of attendant light, the vestige of an existence otherwise obliterated from our memories. As we move forward into life, this recollection fades; maturity, with its habits and its cares and its increase of distance from our celestial origin, causes the glory to diminish. Nothing could be more poignantly sad than the conclusion of this part with the heavy sonority of its last line:

> Full soon thy Soul shall have her earthly freight,
> And custom lie upon thee with a weight,
> Heavy as frost, and deep almost as life!

Between this movement of despair and the following movement of hope there is no clear connection save that of contradiction. But between the question itself and the movement of hope there is an explicit verbal link, for the question is: "Whither has *fled* the visionary gleam?" and the movement of hope answers that

> nature yet remembers
> What was so *fugitive.*

The second movement of the second part of the "Ode" tells us again what has happened to the visionary gleam: it has not wholly fled. This possession of childhood has been passed on as a legacy to the child's heir, the adult man; for the mind, as the "Rainbow" epigraph also says, is one and continuous, and what was so intense a light in childhood becomes "the fountain light of all our day" and "a master light of all our seeing."

But what is this fountain light, this master light? I am sure that when we understand it we shall see that the glory Wordsworth means is very different from Coleridge's glory, which is Joy. Wordsworth says that what he holds in memory as the heritage of childhood is exactly *not* the Joy of childhood; not "delight," not "liberty," not even "hope"; not for these, he says, "I raise/ The song of thanks and praise." For what then does he raise it? For this experience of childhood:

> . . . those obstinate questionings
> Of sense and outward things,
> Fallings from us, vanishings;
> Blank misgivings of a Creature
> Moving about in worlds not realised.

He mentions other reasons for gratitude, but here for the moment I should like to halt the enumeration. We are told that light and glory consist, at least in part, of "questionings" and "blank misgivings" in a world not yet *made real,* for surely Wordsworth uses the word "realised" in its most literal sense. In his note on the poem Wordsworth has this to say of the experience he refers to:

> . . . I was often unable to think of external things as having external existence, and I communed with all that I saw as something not apart from, but inherent in, my own material nature. Many times while going to school have I grasped at a wall or tree to recall myself from this abyss of idealism to the reality. At that time I was afraid of such processes.

He remarks that the experience is not peculiar to himself, which is of course true, and he says that it was connected in his thought with a potency of spirit which made him believe that he could never die.

The precise and naturalistic way in which Wordsworth talks of this experience of childhood must cast doubt on Professor Garrod's statement that Wordsworth believed quite literally in the notion of preexistence. Wordsworth is very careful to delimit the extent of his belief; he says that it is "too shadowy a notion to be recommended to faith" as an evidence of immortality; he says that he is using the idea to illuminate another idea—using it, he says, "for my purpose" and "as a poet." It has as much validity for him as any "popular" religious idea might have, that is to say a kind of suggestive validity. We may regard it as a very serious conceit, vested with relative belief, intended to give a high value to the natural experience of the "vanishings." [4]

The naturalistic tone of Wordsworth's note suggests that we shall be doing no violence to the experience of the "vanishings" if we consider it scientifically. In a well-known essay, "Stages in the Development of the Sense of Reality," the Freudian psychologist Ferenczi speaks of the child's reluctance to distinguish between himself and the world and of the slow growth of ob-

[4] In his *Studies in the Poetry of Henry Vaughan,* a Cambridge University dissertation, Andrew Chiappe makes a similar judgment of the quality and degree of belief in the idea of preëxistence in the poetry of Vaughan and Traherne.

jectivity which differentiates between the ego and external things. And Freud himself, dealing in the language of his own science with the "oceanic" sensation of "being at one with the universe," which a literary friend had supposed to be the source of all religious emotions, conjectures that it is a vestige of the infant's state of feeling before he has learned to distinguish between the stimuli of his own sensations and those of the world outside. Freud says in part:

Originally the ego includes everything, later it detaches from itself the outside world. The ego-feeling we are aware of now is thus only a shrunken vestige of a more extensive feeling—a feeling which embraced the universe and expressed an inseparable connection of the ego with the external world. If we may suppose that this primary ego-feeling has been preserved in the minds of many people —to a greater or lesser extent—it would co-exist like a sort of counterpart with the narrower and more sharply outlined ego-feeling of maturity, and the ideational content belonging to it would be precisely the notion of limitless extension and oneness with the universe—the same feeling as that described by my friend as "oceanic" [*Civilization and Its Discontents*, pp. 13–14].

This, it seems to me, is what Wordsworth is referring to in the "Ode" when he speaks of "worlds not realised." But Wordsworth was very much interested in reality, and, like Freud, he knew that the child's way of apprehension was but a stage which in the course of nature would have to give way to another. If we understand that Wordsworth is speaking of a period common

to the development of everyone, we are helped to see
that we cannot identify the vision of that period with
his peculiar poetic power.

But in addition to the experience of the "vanishings" there is another experience for which Wordsworth is grateful to his childhood and which, I believe,
goes with the "vanishings" to make up the "master
light," the "fountain light." I am not referring to the

> High instincts before which our mortal Nature
> Did tremble like a guilty Thing surprised,

but rather to what Wordsworth calls "those first af-
fections." I am inclined to think that with this phrase
Wordsworth refers to a later stage in the child's development which, like the earlier stage in which the
external world is included within the ego, leaves ves-
tiges in the developing mind.[5] I mean that period described in a well-known passage in Book II of *The
Prelude* in which the child learns about the world in
his mother's arms:

> Blest the infant Babe,
> (For with my best conjecture I would trace
> Our Being's earthly progress,) blest the Babe,
> Nursed in his Mother's arms, who sinks to sleep,
> Rocked on his Mother's breast; who with his soul
> Drinks in the feelings of his Mother's eye!
> For him, in one dear Presence, there exists

---

[5] I am not perfectly sure that Wordsworth is referring to three
different kinds of experience in lines 142–50; very possibly there is
only one experience, the "vanishings," and all the passage refines on
this. But I think that there can be no doubt that the "vanishings"
are connected with the experience of learning to which I now refer.

A virtue which irradiates and exalts
Objects, through widest intercourse of sense.
No outcast he, bewildered and depressed:
Along his infant veins are interfused
The gravitation and the filial bond
Of nature that connect him with the world.
Is there a flower, to which he points with hand
Too weak to gather it, already love
Drawn from love's purest earthly fount for him
Hath beautified that flower; already shades
Of pity cast from inward tenderness
Do fall around him upon aught that bears
Unsightly marks of violence or harm.
Emphatically such a Being lives,
Frail creature as he is, helpless as frail,
An inmate of this active universe:
For feeling has to him imparted power
That through the growing faculties of sense,
Doth like an agent of the one great Mind
Create, creator and receiver both,
Working but in alliance with the works
Which it beholds.—Such, verily is the first
Poetic [6] spirit of our human life,
By uniform control of after years,
In most, abated or suppressed; in some,
Through every change of growth and of decay,
Pre-eminent till death.

The child, this passage says, does not perceive things
merely as objects; he first sees them, because maternal
love is a condition of his perception, as objects-and-
judgments, as valued-objects. He does not learn about

[6] The use here of the word "poetic" might seem to make identical
this way of seeing and the writing of poetry. I think, however, that
Wordsworth is using the word "poetic" metaphorically, not literally.

a flower, but about the flower-that-I-want, about the pretty-flower. The safety, warmth, and good feeling of his mother's conscious benevolence is a circumstance of his first learning. He sees, in short, with "glory"; not only is he himself not in "utter nakedness" as the "Ode" puts it, but the objects he sees are not in "utter nakedness." The passage from *The Prelude* puts in naturalistic language what stanza v of the "Ode" puts into a theistical metaphor. Both the *Prelude* passage and the "Ode" distinguish a state of "exile" from a state of security and comfort, of at-homeness, and both conclude that though the increase of maturity diminishes the perfect sense of at-homeness, there is (as the *Prelude* passage puts it) a "filial bond" or (as in stanza x of the "Ode") a "primal sympathy" which keeps man from being an "outcast . . . bewildered and depressed."

The "Ode" and *The Prelude* differ about the source of this primal sympathy or filial bond; the "Ode" makes heavenly preëxistence the source, *The Prelude* finds the source in maternal affection. But we may remember that the psychologists tell us that notions of heavenly preëxistence figure commonly as representations of physical prenatality; the womb is the environment which is perfectly adapted to its inmate, and compared to it all other conditions of life may well seem like "exile" to the (very literal) "outcast." Even the security of the mother's arms, though it is an effort to recreate for the child the old environment, is but a diminished comfort. And if we think of the other experience of which Wordsworth is speaking, the "vanishings," as the child's recollection of a condition in which it was very nearly true that he and his environment were one, it will not seem surprising that Wordsworth should compound the two experiences and figure them in the single metaphor of the glorious heavenly preëxistence.[7]

I have tried to be as naturalistic as possible in speaking of Wordsworth's childhood experiences and the quasi-Platonic idea they suggested to him. I have done so for no other purpose than to come to a clearer understanding of the intention of the "Ode." For what we must now see is that Wordsworth is talking about something common to us all, the development of the sense of reality. To have once had the visionary gleam is necessary for the process of our human nature, and it is therefore connected with the making of poetry; but it is not in itself the poetry-making power, and its diminution is right and inevitable. That there should be an ambivalence in Wordsworth's response to this change is quite natural, and the two answers, stanzas v–viii and stanzas ix–xi, comprise both the resistance to and the acceptance of growth; inevitably we resist change and turn passionately back to the stage we are leaving; still, we fulfill ourselves by choosing what is

---

[7] Readers of Ferenczi's remarkable study, *Thalassa,* a discussion, admittedly speculative, but wonderfully fascinating, of unconscious racial memories of the ocean as the ultimate source of life, will not be able to resist giving an added meaning to Wordsworth's lines about the "immortal sea/ Which brought us hither" and of the unborn children who "sport upon the shore."

painful and difficult, and we develop by moving toward death: in short, organic development is a hard paradox which Wordsworth is stating in the discrepant answers of the second part of the "Ode."

To speak naturalistically of Wordsworth's experiences does not in the least diminish the value he attached to them, for despite its dominating theistical metaphor, the "Ode" is wholly naturalistic in its intention. What that intention is may be learned from the juxtaposition of the phrase "Foster-child" (line 82) with the word "imperial" (line 84). "Imperial," which finds its echo in "the inevitable yoke" and the "Slave" of stanza viii, suggests pomp, grandeur, dignity, and splendor, all the opposites of what, in *The Excursion,* Wordsworth was to call "littleness." "Littleness" is the result of having wrong notions of the nature of man and of his connection with the universe; its outcome is "deadness." The melancholy and despair of the Solitary in *The Excursion* are the signs of the deadness which resulted from his having conceived of man as something less than imperial. Wordsworth's idea of splendid power is his protest against all views of the mind that would limit and debase it. By conceiving, as he does, an intimate connection between mind and universe, by seeing the universe fitted to the mind and the mind to the universe, he bestows upon man a dignity which cannot be derived from looking at him in the actualities of politics and morals.

Yet here again we must credit Wordsworth with the awareness of tragic paradox. Man must be conceived of

as "imperial," but he must also be seen as he actually
is in the field of life, in politics and morals. The earth
is not an environment in which the celestial or imperial qualities can easily exist. Wordsworth, who
speaks of the notion of imperial preëxistence as being
adumbrated by Adam's fall, uses the words "earth" and
"earthly" in the common quasi-religious sense to refer
to the things of this world; he does not make Earth
synonymous with Nature, for though man may be the
true child of Nature, he is the "foster-child" of Earth.

Wordsworth, in short, is looking at man in a double
way; he is seeing man in his ideal nature and in his
earthly activity. The two views do not so much contradict as supplement each other. If in stanzas v–viii
Wordsworth tells us that we live by decrease, in stanzas
ix–xi he tells us of the everlasting connection of the
diminished person with his own ideal personality. The
child hands on to the hampered adult the imperial
nature, the

. . . primal sympathy
Which having been must ever be,

the mind fitted to the universe, the universe to the
mind. The sympathy is not so intense in maturity as in
childhood, but only because another relation grows up
beside the relation of man to Nature; the relation of
man to his fellows in the moral world of difficulty and
pain. Given Wordsworth's subjective epistemology,
the new relation is bound to change the very aspect of
Nature itself: the clouds will take a sober coloring

from an eye that hath kept watch o'er man's mortality, but a sober color is a color still.

There is sorrow in the "Ode," the inevitable sorrow of giving up an old habit of vision for a new one. In shifting the center of his interest from Nature to morality Wordsworth is fulfilling his own conception of the three ages of man which Professor Beatty has expounded so well. The shift in interest he called the coming of "the philosophic mind," and it is surely sentimental to say that Wordsworth believed that this was only second best, a falling away from the poetic mind; for Wordsworth the poetic mind and the philosophic mind are the same. Nor is it any less sentimental to say that because Wordsworth sees the world under the aspect of the

> . . . sober colouring from an eye
> That hath kept watch o'er man's mortality,

he is less a man and less a poet. He is only less a youth.

The "Ode," then, is not a dirge, and if it be a farewell it is not a farewell to the poetic power. The poetic power is, as a matter of fact, not mentioned in the "Ode" at all; yet it is there by implication, for the "Ode" ends with the poet's dedication of himself to a new kind of interest, really a new poetic subject. Yet if the "Ode" is not a farewell to poetry, was there not, after its composition, a great falling off in Wordsworth's genius? There was, indeed, although the decline is not so sharp as is commonly held and although it must be remembered how another statement of the loss of the visionary gleam, that of "Tintern Abbey," had been followed by the superb production of the "great decade." [8] But a diminution there undoubtedly was, and how are we to account for it? Well, perhaps we shall be most scientific by abstaining from science. It is not impossible, ideally speaking, to make the explanation, but any account of why Wordsworth ceased writing great poetry must at the same time be an account of how he once *did* write great poetry; I submit that in the present state of our knowledge of the human mind we cannot furnish that account.

I do not think that criticism can do what science cannot do, but criticism can at least suggest the magnitude of the task at which Wordsworth failed. Had Wordsworth fulfilled the terms of his dedication, he would, as I conceive it, have turned away from what Keats called the "egotistical sublime" and turned toward tragic poetry in order to express the "thoughts that do often lie too deep for tears"; had he done so and had he succeeded with it in as high degree as he had succeeded with subjective poetry, his achievement would have been almost unthinkable. Temperamentally he was barred from tragedy; that special form of strong feeling which by habit we call "objectivity" he did not have. In this he was a man of his time, for it was com-

8 This fact is sometimes dealt with by saying that Wordsworth wrote his best work from his near memories of the "gleam" and that as he grew older and moved further from it, his recollection of it dimmed and thus he lost his power. This makes a strange conception of the poetic process, and it does not extricate from the toils of their usual mechanical notion of the mind those who speculate on Wordsworth's decline.

mon to all the romantic poets from Wordsworth to Arnold that they should desire and be unable to achieve dramatic "objectivity." The "Negative Capability" which Keats believed was the source of Shakespeare's power, the gift of being able to remain "content with half-knowledge" was hard to come by for the poets of the nineteenth century. What this "Capability" negates is not philosophic thought, but only "an irritable reaching after fact and reason"; it suggests that there are circumstances in which "half-knowledge" is the fuller knowledge and one is most truly philosophical by remaining "in uncertainties, mysteries, doubts."

Well, this capability Wordsworth did not have; the theological habit asserted itself above the dramatic. Had the theology been complete, Wordsworth might have seen with a Dantesque vision; had it been passionate, he might have seen with a Miltonic; but it was neither complete nor passionate. And when we have said even as much as this we have perhaps touched the borders of speculation and said too much.

In this essay I have undertaken only to remove certain preconceptions concerning the intention of the "Ode: Intimations of Immortality" and to state what I believe to be the actual intention of the poem. This, in a way, is a job of archaeology; it has been dictated, not by any theory of the proper way to "approach" poetry in general—on an occasion like this it is proper for me to say that I am in possession of no such theory —but only by my sense of what this particular poem requires of criticism at this particular time.